CLAMMING

The Pacific Northwest Coast

Ken Axt

www.razorclamming.com

Frank Amato Publications

This book is designed to provide information and motivation to our readers. It is sold with the understanding that the writer, Ken Axt, the website, www.razorclamming.com, the company WebRazorDesign and the publishers are not engaged to render any type of up-to-date information on state and federal regulations, the safety and instruction of handling, cleaning, cooking and consumption of shellfish. No warranties or guarantees are expressed or implied on any of the content in this volume. You are responsible for your own choices, actions and results when digging, cleaning, cooking and consuming shellfish.

Always check with the Oregon Department of Fish and Wildlife at www.dfw.state.or.us and Washington Department of Fish and Wildlife at www.wdfw.wa.gov for up-to-date regulations, closures of clamming locations, levels of toxins, red tides and other pollutions that can make shellfish unsafe for consumption.

Some of the product names and company names used in the book have been used for identification purposes and may be trademarks or registered trademarks of their respective manufacturers and sellers.

Book & Map Design: Esther Poleo
Photographs: Ken Axt

FRANK AMATO PUBLICATIONS, INC.
All inquiries should be addressed to:
PO Box 82112, Portland, Oregon 97282   (503) 653-8108 AmatoBooks.com
Softbound ISBN-978-157188-527-2 Softbound UPC: 0-81127-00380-8
Printed in Singapore

ACKNOWLEDGMENTS

Grant Howard, Gene Axt and Nate Axt

This book is dedicated to my nephew, Grant Howard. Without Grant's companionship and support this book would never have been written. His curiosity and enthusiasm for clamming was a constant motivator and made this endeavor fun. Most importantly, he spent hours filming and taking photos for both the www.razorclamming.com website and this book.

To my son, Nate Axt, we've spent our lives digging, cooking and eating Razor Clams together. My uncle, Gene Axt, with whom I've enjoyed Seaside, Oregon since 1963, and the network of his friends at the coast who have all been invaluable resources for this book.

Last, a thank you to Oregon Department of Fish and Wildlife and Washington Department of Fish & Wildlife for their websites and their collective efforts preserving this time-honored tradition for all of us!

CONTENTS

INTRODUCTION 7

RAZOR CLAMS 8

Harvesting Razor Clams 11
Best Beaches for Razor Clamming 12
Great Beginner Spots 13
When to Go Razor Clamming 16
How to Read A Tide Book 17
Identifying Razor Clam Shows 18
Five Ways to Find Clam Shows 20
How to Dig Razor Clams 24
Razor Clamming At Night 32
Should I Use Razor Clam Shovel or Gun? 36
Razor Clamming Clothing 42
Is Razor Clamming A Sport or Hobby? 47

Cleaning Your Razor Clams   49
Storing Razor Clams   52
Razor Clam Recipes   54

BAY CLAMS   59
Best Oregon Bays   61
Best Washington Bays   62
Bay Clam Details & Shows   65
How to Dig Bay Clams   67
Cleaning Bay Clams   71
Clean or Purge?   73
Bay Clam Recipes   77

MORE ON TIDES   79
SHELLFISH SPECIES AND REGULATIONS   81
CLAMMING LOCATIONS   83

DEDICATION

To My Family….

It all started one spring morning in 1964 in Seaside, Oregon. My grandfather rustled us kids out of bed at dawn. We made our way over the grassy dunes and down to the ocean shore. Dressed in his fishing waders, with a Razor Clamming shovel in one hand and a bag in the other, our grandfather slowly walked along the water's edge, pounding the sand with the butt of his shovel, and then it happened–a small hole appeared in the wet sand and in a matter of seconds he had dug and scooped up an Oregon Coast delicacy. There he knelt on one knee, showing us for the first time a big, beautiful, water-squirting Razor Clam! We were hooked after that and spent the many years to come with friends and family, Razor Clamming the Pacific Northwest Coast.

Many decades have passed but those fond memories remain, as if they had just happened yesterday. Now I'm the one waking the kids up early in the morning, taking them over those same dunes, shovel in hand, on our way down to the morning shore in excited pursuit of those beautiful "Razors". Although, that's not really why we get together, we are here to spend time together as a family. They don't know it yet but when they have families of their own they, too, will look back on these adventures with the joy that I do. And that's what this Razor Clamming business is all about: Spending time with your loved ones!

Ken Axt

"Digging Razor Clams together connects our family's past to our future."

INTRODUCTION

In 1961, my grandparents purchased the Harmony Courts Motel on 9th Street and Downing in Seaside, Oregon. I was seven years old and every weekend and summers were spent at the beach. Sunday dinners were generally Razor Clams, which started a family tradition of digging these clams that continues to this day. I am sixty now and all of these great family memories have motivated me to write this book, in hopes of other families enjoying these experiences, too.

I am not a writer, marine biologist or commercial Razor Clammer. I spent my career in the computer industry and have traveled around the world. Everywhere I went I was interested in the local shellfish because of my experiences on the Oregon and Washington coasts. On these trips I have discovered and enjoyed many shellfish delicacies. But for me, none measure up to the Pacific Northwest Razor Clam.

If you are not a marine biologist or commercial fisherman, this book is written for you. I do not spend a lot of time on terms like Siliqua patula, Phylum mollusca or Bivalve (scientific name for clams, oysters, scallops and mussels). Instead, I do my best to share why you might want to get interested in clamming and how to get started, without all the technical jargon. Or, if you are an experienced clammer, how you might increase your skill level and broaden your experiences with other species of clams and new locations.

Please remember that this is a treasured Pacific Northwest resource. Together we must manage it so generations to come will be able to enjoy gathering, cleaning and eating this succulent delicacy for many years to come.

Happy Tides!

Ken Axt

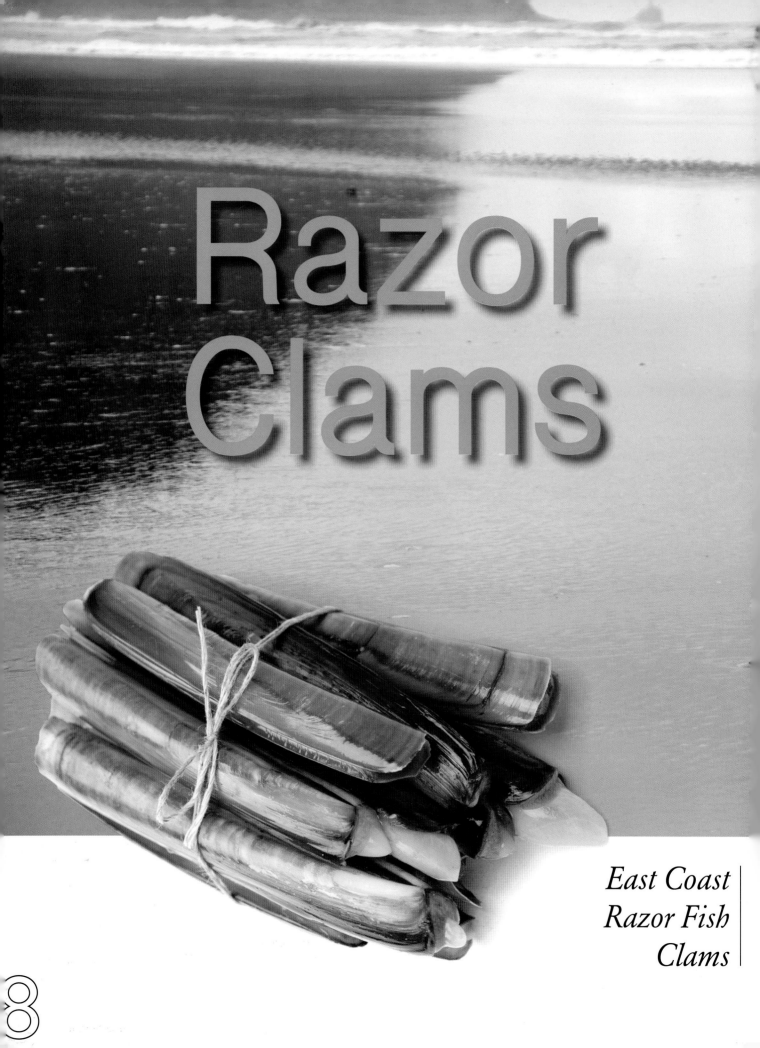

Razor Clams

East Coast Razor Fish Clams

The Pacific Northwest Coast is one of the most environmentally protected coastlines in the world.

Oregon has the most widely accessible beaches; Long Beach in Washington is also a great spot, and is arguably the longest drivable beach in the world. These beaches, and more than 400 bays and estuaries, offer some of the most fertile clamming beds in North America.

The most popular clam by far is the Pacific Northwest Razor Clam and I believe it is one of our region's best-kept secrets.

Abalone is delicious, but it sells for up to $125 a pound. Harvesting is very difficult, and that's if you can find them! The taste is very similar to a Razor Clam but the Razor Clam has a digger, which is more tender and tasty than an Abalone. Razor Clams are also in good supply and are easily harvested.

In Asia the Pacific Northwest Geoduck (pronounced gooey-duck) sells for up to $300 per clam, in part because the Asians believe it has aphrodisiac qualities. Geoducks are not easily found or harvested. Forty years ago Geoducks in the Pacific Northwest were cheap and generally chopped up for clam chowder. Today, they are mostly used in sushi and very rarely fried whole. They call the Geoduck the "King of Clams" because they are huge, with some up to 160 years old and six feet long. However, there are a lot of people that don't like Sushi and even though I like Sushi, I don't like Geoduck Sushi. I do not care for the flavor of the non-neck meat either. For me, the Razor Clam is King because of its availability, delicate flavor and tenderness.

The Pacific Northwest Razor Clam is in abundance and for the most part all you need to harvest them is a shellfish license, shovel and a bucket. With a limit of fifteen per person, a family of four can take sixty in a day, enough for three or four fantastic family meals and all for the cost of a shellfish license. I grew up not just eating Razor Clams but these other now-rare shellfish eatables as well. In fact, in the 1960's sometimes we had so much abalone we fed it to our dogs!

The better part of the last forty years I spent my career traveling the globe—Canada, Mexico, France, Britain, Israel (even in Jerusalem you can find fresh shellfish). No matter where I went, I was always interested in experiencing local shellfish. I would ask people if they had ever tried a Pacific Northwest Razor

Abalone

Northwest Razor Clam

Clam and, without fail, I got the same answer, "Oh, yeah, those little round things." Nobody even knew what a Razor Clam looked like.

There are close relatives to the Pacific Razor Clam found around the world but none can compare with the large, thick, flavorful Pacific Razor Clam. For example, on the East Coast you'll find Razor Fish Clams (same family as the Pacific Razor Clam), also called Jackknife Clams, and they can be found on the Northern European Coast too. There are other clam varieties in China, Australia, Chile, Peru, Argentina, and more. You will rarely see Razor Fish Clams and these other variants fried whole, like you would a Pacific Northwest Razor Clam (filleted and opened flat like a steak). They are too small and narrow, so they are prepared like steamer clams or in a wine sauce or sometimes as clam strips. They are good but, in my opinion, not nearly as good as a Pacific Northwest Razor Clam.

People outside of the Pacific Northwest don't know they exist, but many Oregonians don't even know that Razor Clams are found on our own beaches!

If you are a local Razor Clammer you cannot imagine paying $100 to $200 per pound for a Pacific Northwest Razor Clam. But it's only a matter of time before demand outgrows availability. In fact, they farm Abalone in California and now Geoducks in Washington. Scientists are now experimenting with farming Razor Clams too.

Harvesting Razor Clams

Happy Razor Clammers: Nate, Grant, Gene with skillful clamming Annie from Seaside, Oregon.

The Razor Clam is the most commonly harvested clams in the Pacific Northwest. Clamming is an inexpensive family activity that all ages can enjoy. With an easy-to-use Razor Clam gun on the wet sand, even beginner Razor Clammers can be successful on their very first day!

Veteran Razor Clammers will tell you they love the sport of it. For them, the challenge of Razor Clamming in the surf (instead of the wet sand) is a matter of pride and status. In the surf, you use a swifter clam shovel instead of a Razor Clam gun. The butt of the shovel is used to pound the surf, this causes Razor Clam "shows" (the impression they leave in the sand when their neck is withdrawn). A Razor Clam will dig downward faster in the surf (up to a foot in seconds), so it's challenging and takes time and practice to learn. But in the surf, results can mean quicker and more frequent limits, and larger Razor Clams.

There is nothing quite like standing in the ocean surf on a beautiful summer day, enjoying the company of your fellow Razor Clammers (hence the phrase, "Happy Clammer".)

Once harvested, the Razor Clam is easy to clean, has a very high percentage of edible meat and makes for a fantastic meal.

Best Beaches for Razor Clamming

Razor Clams can be found on beaches all along the Pacific Coast. However, because they live in inter-tidal ocean beach areas with shifting sands and unstable surf, this causes difficulty in reproduction. Like many sea creatures, eggs and sperm are released in the water for fertilization to occur. Areas with frequently changing currents, water temperatures and fluctuating predator populations (Dungeness crab love razor clams) can make it seriously difficult for free-swimming larvae to survive. Consequently, some areas have stable Razor Clam populations, while others can change year to year.

Today, the 18-mile stretch of beach from Tillamook head in Seaside to Clatsop Spit on the Columbia River is where more than 90% of Razor Clams are harvested in Oregon. The 28 miles of beach in Long Beach, Washington is where more than 90% of Razor Clams are harvested in Washington. In these two areas, as many as five-million Razor Clams can be harvested in a good year.

There are no reliable Razor Clam sources in the Puget Sound, Washington area. However, there are other productive areas north of Long Beach, as well as south of Seaside to California. There are a number of additional beach areas with Razor Clams that aren't listed, mostly because their populations and availability varies greatly from year to year based on less favorable inter-tidal beach conditions, which can make consistent reproduction difficult.

Below is a list of where most of the Razor Clams are dug in the Pacific Northwest.

RAZOR CLAMMING BEACHES	SEASIDE, OREGON NORTH TO COLUMBIA RIVER	Cannon Beach	Short Sands—Manzanita	Cape Meares Beach	Agate Beach	Newport—North Beach	Newport—South Beach	Waldport Beach	Bandon—Whiskey Run	Meyers Creek—Gold Beach	LONG BEACH, WASHINGTON	Twin Harbors	Copalis Beach	Mocrocks	Kalaloch
	90% of Oregon Clams are Dug Here	OR	OR	OR	OR	OR	OR	OR	OR	OR	90% of WA Clams are Dug Here	WA	WA	WA	WA

Great Beginner Spots

Commercial Razor Clammers know where the Razor Clams are.

Both Seaside, Oregon and Long Beach, Washington are great places for beginners. Seaside Razor Clamming is open all year with the exception of ten weeks in the fall. Washington has fewer open dates and they are posted just a few months, or less, in advance. Check "Shellfish Species and Regulations" (page 86) to get Oregon's Razor Clamming season dates, and visit the Oregon Department of Fish and Wildlife website www.dfw.state.or.us. For Washington's dates, refer to the Washington Department of Fish and Wildlife website www.wdfw.wa.gov.

SEASIDE is just 80 miles west of Portland, Oregon. It is also one of the most beautiful beaches on the West Coast and is widely known for great Razor Clamming. You'll also find licenses, tide charts and equipment conveniently located in nearby stores, gas stations, outdoor and tackle shops, etc. If you stay over, most hotels are within walking distance of everything you'll need. In the morning just walk down to the beach and go clamming…easy peasy!

When in Seaside, I frequently go straight down Avenue G to the beach. Sometimes it's best to follow the herd; many times you'll see groups of people following locals that know where the clams are. If you see people bending over digging clams, you're in the right spot. If you don't see anyone digging, the further out the sand goes prior to hitting the surf the better. If you don't have luck in one spot, start moving up and down the beach.

Often, if I don't find anything after an hour or so, I will move down the beach and catch my limit in twenty minutes. So be patient, enjoy the day and your chances for success will increase significantly.

Occasionally you might spot a commercial Razor Clammer, easily distinguished by the huge bag of Razor Clams dragging in the surf behind them. There are no limits for commercial Razor Clammers and these guys are doing it for a living so if they are there, the Razor Clamming is probably as good as it gets.

These commercial clammers are hard at work and are pretty serious about going about their business. But, in general, recreational clammers are always

helpful when asked. When I get my limit I often like to find beginning clammers along the beach and help them spot clam "shows" in the wet sand. I see lots of other veteran clammers do this from time to time, too! So don't hesitate to ask others how they are doing, you can learn a lot by talking to other clammers on the beach.

LONG BEACH, Washington is just 100 miles west from Portland and 150 miles from Tacoma, Washington. Washington has been using Razor Clam population best practices since 1948. That is when they discontinued their annual Long Beach Razor Clam Festival, which offered free fried clams cooked in the "World's Largest Frying Pan". They believed that the popularity of the clam festival was dwindling the Razor Clam population so they began managing it, mostly by restricting the number of available days and by providing less notice to clammers. Many believe that because there are fewer days to harvest Razor Clams the clamming is better and the clams get larger. A few years back they even reopened the yearly clam festival. The April event date is posted almost a year in advance, for more information go to: www.longbeachrazorclamfestival.com.

Other Pacific Razor Clamming areas are discussed later in the book.

Seaside, Oregon is a great place for beginners to start.

When to Go
Razor Clamming

Tides are very important! The further out the surf, the more likely Razor Clamming will be good. Tide books are available at most sporting goods stores and once you're at the beach, you'll find them at most stores and gas stations.

Be sure you check the proper tide book or website, they focus on different locations, so be sure to check the tides specific to the area where you will be clamming. Depending on where you pick up the tide book, it will be built around the closest tide-data monitoring station. In Portland, tide-data monitors (which collect historical tide data) are located around the Willamette and Columbia rivers, which is a long way from the coast. Portland river tides can have more than a two-hour difference from ocean beach tides. Even a Long Beach tide can be 30 minutes different from a Seaside tide.

The intertidal zone midpoint between "High" and "Low" tide is "0". Clamming is best on a lower minus (-0.1) tide and worse on a higher (0.1) plus tide.

Since we harvest Razor Clams only in the intertidal zone, tides that are -2.0 (two feet lower than the mid "0" point) or more are as good as it gets. However, depending on other factors (see "More On Tides," on page 79), you can limit out on a plus tide (0.4), when other conditions are just right. So any minus tide is better but it doesn't have to be the lowest tide, depending on other conditions (weather, tidal surge, etc.). In general, look for a tide somewhere between 0.4 and -2.0 or lower.

Since Razor Clam shows appear more often on the outgoing tide, it becomes more challenging when the tide turns and starts coming in. So, be there two hours early and clam following the surf out as it reaches the lowest point of the tide.

To find accurate Razor Clam tide information go to www.razorclamming.com/tide-tables/. This tide data is focused on Seaside's Tillamook Head to Long Beach, Washington and is specifically for Razor Clamming.

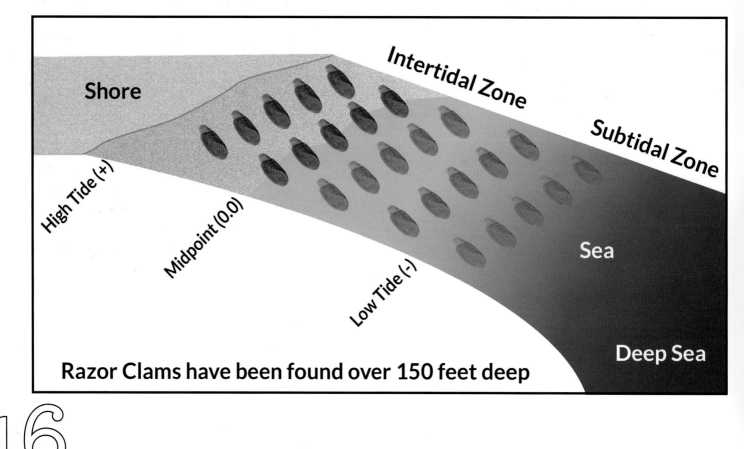

Shore · Intertidal Zone · Subtidal Zone · High Tide (+) · Midpoint (0.0) · Low Tide (-) · Sea · Deep Sea

Razor Clams have been found over 150 feet deep

How to Read a Tide Book

JUNE TIDES

Date	Time	Ht. Feet	Time	Ht. Feet	Time	Ht. Feet	Time	Ht. Feet
	AM			**NOON**			**PM**	
1 M	12:41a	H 8.5	**6:59a**	**L -0.7**	1:20p	H 7.6	7:04p	L 0.7 ○
2 Tu	1:23a	H 8.7	**7:48a**	**L -1.0**	2:12p	H 7.5	7:40p	L 0.1
3 W	2:03a	H 8.7	**8:35a**	**L -1.1**	3:04p	H 7.3	8:33p	L 1.5
4 Th	2:44a	H 8.5	**9:21a**	**L -0.9**	3:55p	H 7.1	9:18p	L 2.0
5 F	3:26a	H 8.2	**10:08a**	**L -0.5**	4:48p	H 6.7	10:04p	L 2.4 ●
6 Sa	4:10a	H 7.7	10:56a	L 0.0	5:42p	H 6.4	10:55p	L 2.9
7 Su	4:59a	H 7.1	11:48a	L 0.4	6:40p	H 6.1	11:54p	L 3.2

Tide books can be complicated to read. First, find the month and dates you plan on going clamming. Notice above there are four tides per day, two low tides and two high tides. Let's say you wanted to go the first week of June. You're in luck, low minus tides Monday through Friday, to June 5th. The more "negative" the tide is, the easier the clamming is going to be because more of the intertidal zone is exposed and the more readily available the clams will be.

The lowest tide for the week is a -1.1, on Wednesday, June 3rd at 8:35 a.m. (highlighted and circled in red). Remember the time listed is at its lowest point and all tide charts can be off a little bit. It's ideal to be two hours early and clam on the outgoing tide. You can still go clamming on the incoming tide but razor clam "shows" are much better on the outgoing tide.

So try and be on the beach at least 1 hour (2 hours is best) before low tide, otherwise you will miss the outgoing tide.

There are many factors that determine how clams will show (weather, tidal surge, water temperature, etc.). Even a full moon can positively affect how the clams are showing. Notice the moon icon indicating a full moon on Friday (on the right of the chart). So, although that -1.1 tide has the most promise, if the weather looks to be better on Friday, June 5th and other conditions fall into place, the clams could be showing better on Friday. If the conditions are right, I would even go on Sunday, June 7th with a non-minus 0.4 tide. This entire week has promise.

For more information on tides, see "More On Tides" chapter on page 79.

Identifying Razor Clam Shows

A Razor Clam "show" is created by the impression the clam leaves in the sand when its neck is withdrawn. On a perfect day, in a perfect surf, with a perfect tide, Razor Clam shows are easy to find. On rare occasion, you can even see their necks sticking out of the surf, this is called "necking." I've seen a group of Razor Clams perfectly necking once in my lifetime. On a typical day, spotting Razor Clam shows is a little more challenging and spotting them is what separates those that consistently limit and those that don't.

EXAMPLES OF COMMON RAZOR CLAM SHOWS

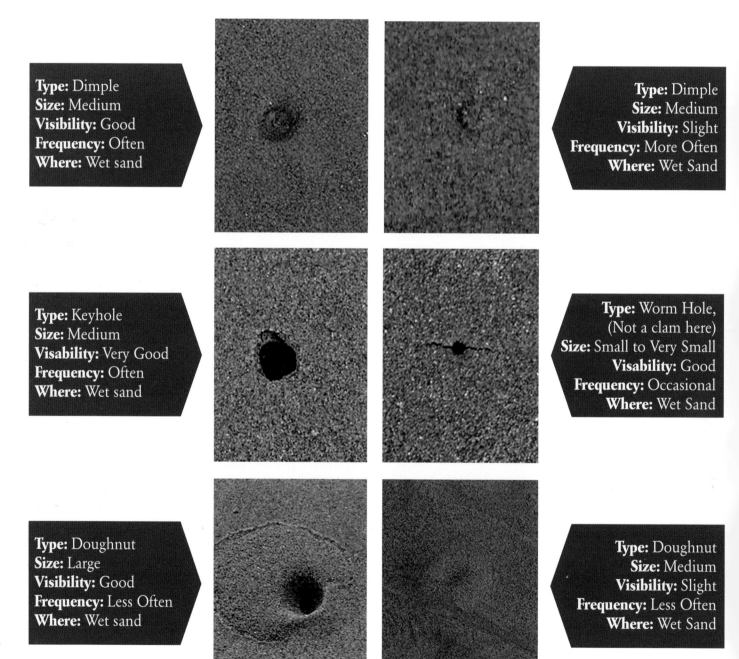

Type: Dimple
Size: Medium
Visibility: Good
Frequency: Often
Where: Wet sand

Type: Dimple
Size: Medium
Visibility: Slight
Frequency: More Often
Where: Wet Sand

Type: Keyhole
Size: Medium
Visability: Very Good
Frequency: Often
Where: Wet sand

Type: Worm Hole,
(Not a clam here)
Size: Small to Very Small
Visability: Good
Frequency: Occasional
Where: Wet Sand

Type: Doughnut
Size: Large
Visibility: Good
Frequency: Less Often
Where: Wet sand

Type: Doughnut
Size: Medium
Visibility: Slight
Frequency: Less Often
Where: Wet Sand

Type: Surf Runoff
Clam Necking "V"
Size: Medium
Visibility: Temporary
Frequency: Seldom
Where: Surf runoff

Type: Tiny Rock,
(Not a clam here)
Size: Small-Medium
Visibility: Good
Frequency: Occasionally
Where: Wet Sand

Type: Ocean Surf
Size: Large
Visibility: Very Good
Frequency: Occasional
Where: 6" Slack Surf

Type: Ocean Surf
Size: Small
Visibility: Slight
Frequency: Often
Where: 8" Slack Surf

If You Can't See It, You Can't Dig It

Some clammers look for Razor Clam shows in the wet sand, others in the surf and some look in both. Expect many variations in Razor Clam shows as no two are exactly alike. Shows in the surf will open and close in a matter of seconds. Shows in soft, wet sand seem to be larger in diameter and can protrude more from the sand, making them easier to detect. Razor Clam shows in harder (denser) wet sand are smaller and protrude less, if at all. The Razor Clam's movements, the density of the sand, surf and other variables determine what the show will look like.

On a good day they are easy to see in the wet sand, but on a difficult day they can be very faint and extremely hard to see. In the surf, visibility can be poor, the show can be small and some open and close in less than a second. Developing a keen eye for shows takes practice. But consistently catching your limit depends on your ability to spot the show because, "If you can't see it, you can't dig it!"

Five Ways to Find
Clam Shows

There are a number of ways to find shows, both on wet sand and in the surf. I will discuss the most popular ones, starting with the easiest and most widely used. In general, the conditions of the day influence which approach will work best. Some days shows are easy to find no matter what approach you use. Other days, only one approach seems to garner results. Experienced clammers clam in the surf because, in general, shows are easier to provoke and more reliably found there. As you master each approach, your catch will increase and the time it takes to limit out will decrease. Once you are comfortable with one approach, try not to get stuck on just what you know, master them all. That way when conditions change, no matter which method is most productive you'll be ready. Best of all, you will have become a "Happy Clammer!"

1. Walking Down the Beach

The easiest and most common way to find shows is to walk the beach scanning the wet sand. On a good day, when Razor Clams are feeding, they are easy to spot and you can have your limit in 15 to 20 minutes. More often it takes time, effort and a very keen eye to find even the slightest shows. Keep an eye out for other clammers. If you see a group of people bending over digging, it's a good bet that's where the clams are!

Often there will be nothing showing for an hour or so and then, all of a sudden, they will start feeding and shows can be found everywhere. Be patient, enjoy the day and the beauty of the coast. When they aren't showing at all, try one or more of the following methods.

Walk on the wet sand and look closely to find shows, remember, some will be very slight.

2. Stomping Your Feet

If clams are not feeding, shows are usually barely visible or not visible at all. However, it is possible to make them show by stomping on the wet sand. The stomping creates a disturbance, which provokes the Razor Clams to move, resulting in a show. Some people jump up and down in one spot, others walk down the beach stomping their feet as hard as they can. Keep in mind though that the show might not actually turn up immediately, sometimes it can take a minute or more after you have stomped in the sand. This is because the denser the sand, the slower the clam moves, and the longer it will take for the show to become visible.

Some people stomp in a straight line and if you come upon an area someone has left too soon, you can find shows from their efforts. This is why I stomp in a large circle and take my time to make sure I don't leave any shows behind.

3. Pounding with the Butt of a Razor Clam Shovel

Many people use the butt of a Razor Clamming shovel to pound on the beach or surf. The softer the sand, the more effective this technique is and being closer to the surf it can sometimes be even more rewarding. This is also an effective way to determine whether something that looks like a show (like a worm hole) is actually a Razor Clam show. Pound the butt of your shovel next to the suspected show, this will disrupt the Razor Clam and cause it to shift, move or squirt. This will minimize the time you spend digging worm holes and other false holes.

4. Study the Surf Run-Off

On occasion you will run across Razor Clams during a feeding frenzy. When this happens their necks will stick up and break the surface of the water, this is called "necking". As the water runs past the protruding neck,

Use the butt of the shovel to pound in the surf or wet sand.

Digging for a clam after they found a "V" shape in the ocean surf run off.

it creates a small "V" in the surf run-off. Since they are only seen momentarily, sometimes for just a few seconds, you need a keen eye – and when you spot one you must move quickly so you don't lose sight of the spot where you need to start digging.

Conditions have to be just right to catch Razor Clams feeding like this, so it doesn't happen often. However, if you are lucky enough to stumble upon a feeding frenzy, the clamming will be easy. Some clams will even spit at you. Because they are so close to the surface, pulling them out takes very little effort.

I have had days where I couldn't find shows no matter what I tried. Occasionally I'll spot a clam necking. More frequently, these V's occur even when shows are visible in the wet sand and surf. I recommend that when clamming is good, no matter which approach you use, practice the "V" method because it takes time to get good at spotting them. That way when it's the only way to find shows you will be one of the few people on the beach getting your limit!

5. Ocean Sandbars

Ocean sandbars are like underwater sand dunes that become exposed at low tides. Waves crash against these underwater sandbars, taking little Razor Clam larvae for a ride. When these small, free-riding clams hit the sandbar they attach and dig in for safety. The best sandbars are only exposed at very low tides, but they provide opportunity for both increased size and numbers of Razor Clams.

Of course, along with the increased opportunity comes the requirement for increased skill. You also need to be dressed for the occasion. For example, the woman getting the piggyback ride (see right) has waist waders, which won't help her in the four-foot-deep water hole she needs to cross to get to the sandbar. Luckily, her clamming buddy has chest waders ready for the job.

On occasion, I get so caught up in what I'm doing I forget about the time and rising tide. If the water you have to cross is four feet deep going out and the tide rises a foot while you're out there, it will be five

Ocean sandbars can provide great opportunity and also require more skill.

feet deep coming back to shore. If you're a novice, I recommend sticking to the wet sand. It's best to get comfortable Razor Clamming in the surf. Once you've mastered Razor Clamming in the surf, ocean sandbars will be safer and easier.

SHOW-SIZE MATTERS

It takes about a year for a Razor Clam to grow to three inches. What you are looking for is a Razor Clam that is three years or older, and four to five inches in size. Six-inch Razor Clams are found, and on rare occasion you'll even find some that reach seven inches. I've seen Razor Clams larger than seven inches in both Oregon and Washington. And because of the colder water in Alaska they live longer and can get up to eleven inches! Locally though, the lifespan of a Razor Clam isn't much more than six years so they generally don't get much larger than six inches.

If you are interested in figuring out how old your Razor Clam is, just count the number of color sections on the shell. Each year the newly added growth creates a slightly different color on a Razor Clam's shell. Generally, they grow to about 3 inches the first year, 1 inch the second, then less for each consecutive year.

Remember, you can only keep 15 Razor Clams, so you might not want to dig every show you find. Each clam counts, no matter how small or how badly you cut it up while digging. You don't want to limit out early with 15 clams the size of the one my son Nate is showing here in the picture.

Shows less than a quarter inch in diameter are suspect of being a smaller clam, although the size of the show doesn't always match the size of the clam. With a little time and practice, you'll be able to tell whether it's a large Razor Clam or a small one based on its show. Until then, be mindful of what you dig and keep every clam no matter what its size.

You have to keep every razor clam you dig, no matter how small.

How to Dig Razor Clams

The easiest way to dig a Razor Clam, without breaking it or cutting it in half, is with a gun. Of course, depending on who you talk to, you might get a different opinion. However, I rarely see kids using a shovel and I've never seen a commercial Razor Clammer using a gun.

When you're ready to broaden your skills, learning how to use a shovel in the wet sand is the next step after you're comfortable using a gun. Once you've mastered using a shovel in the wet sand, then moving into the surf will be much easier. Razor Clamming in the surf is more challenging, however, when you get good at doing it you will limit out much more often and with larger clams.

For more information on which style of Razor Clam gun or shovel to use, see "Should I Use a Razor Clam Shovel or Gun?" on page 36.

USING A RAZOR CLAM GUN

Place your gun over the Razor Clam show and make an impression in the sand, raise the gun, step back and adjust as needed.

Since Razor Clams dig vertically and slightly slanted toward the ocean, adjust slightly from center, giving more room on the ocean side.

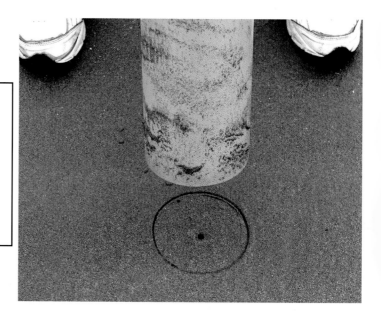

Wiggle the gun a little from side to side and back to front while applying pressure downward. If you bear down, forcing the gun into the sand, an aluminum gun will bend in half. So, wiggle it a little. While descending, try to feel for the Razor Clam. If you hit it, adjust quickly so you don't cut or break the Razor Clam.

There is a hole on the gun handle that releases air as it fills with sand. Place your finger over the hole. The vacuum created by plugging the hole (while you pull upward) will suck the sand and the Razor Clam up out of the sand.

You might get the Razor Clam on the first try if it's close to the surface. If not, repeat the process until you get deep enough.

Move quickly, Razor Clams can dig downward up to three feet deep. Always be mindful of stopping quickly if you hit a clam, and readjust the gun.

If you've gone three feet down and found no clam, look through the sand you've already pulled out, it could be a small one. If it's not in the sand, use your gun or hand to continue digging around the hole (ocean side first) until you find that beautiful water-squirting Razor Clam.

HOW NOT TO USE A RAZOR CLAM SHOVEL

0

One certain way to break or cut your Razor Clam in half is by digging without giving it much thought. This can significantly affect the quality of your take. Frequently we see people with bags of broken and cut-up Razor Clams; we call them "clam chowder" clams! It not only gives away your beginner status but also limits the way you can cook the clams.

Follow the steps below for proper use of a Razor Clam shovel and you'll look like a pro!

HOW TO USE A SHOVEL ON WET SAND

1

Once you find a show, insert the clam shovel about two inches from the ocean side of the show. The trick is to place the shovel's end vertically alongside the clam, keeping in mind the clam is almost vertical, with a slight deviation toward the ocean.

Push the shovel handle downward. This will move the clam into a more horizontal position that keeps it from digging further down in the sand. It will also create a space to slide your hand behind the shovel.

OCEAN ⟶

3

Reach down with your hand and pull the shovel out, positioning your hand as far down into the sand as you can. When the shovel is out, feel around for the Razor Clam. If you don't feel anything, keep going, but gently. The clam might just be a handful of sand away.

4

On light tidal surge days, Razor Clams will be closer to the surface and this method works well. With heavier tidal surges, clams dig deeper and you will have to dig down with your hand or your shovel, sometimes up to 3 feet. If all of the clams are deep, consider using the digging method discussed next.

5

Remember, if you have found a Razor Clam show, the clam is down there somewhere. Don't give up until you pull that water squirting delicacy out of the sand.

ALTERNATIVE APPROACH TO USING A SHOVEL

1

If you find you are breaking Razor Clam shells, give this method a try. This approach allows you to dig a deep hole without breaking or cutting your Razor Clam in half. It's a little more work but well worth the effort to get an unbroken Razor Clam.

2

Keep scooping sand out of the hole, going deeper until you think you're at the depth of the Razor Clam. Because they can be up to three feet deep you might have to feel around with your hands along the way.

3

Use your hand to find the clam. Be careful, especially if you've hit the Razor Clam with your shovel, which can make their edges sharper than usual. I've seen people get cuts or small scrapes, but it's usually because they were overly aggressive. Everyone wants to be the first to get their limit, but it's not worth getting injured for it.

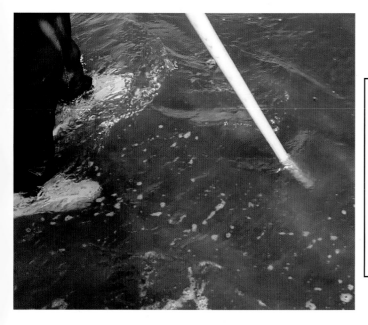

4

Remember, if the show was good, your clam is down there somewhere. Don't give up until you find your Razor Clam! And please help preserve this treasured Pacific Northwest resource for years to come — keep every clam no matter how small.

HOW TO USE A SHOVEL IN THE SURF

1

Slack tide occurs when the surf pauses between going out and coming back in. During that slack-tide moment, it's much easier to see through the water.

Focus on the water that's one to eight inches deep at slack periods. Deeper water makes it more difficult to find and dig shows. Also, the further out you go, larger incoming waves make digging more difficult.

2

Ocean surf sand tends to be softer (looser) than the sand on the beach so you don't have to pound as hard. The show seen here was only open for two seconds before disappearing. Depending on conditions, they can be open a little longer. You have to move quickly to insert your shovel next to the show before it disappears. If you lose sight of it, focus your eyes on where to insert the shovel while you're moving into position.

3

Just like when using your shovel in the wet sand, insert the clam shovel about two inches from the ocean side of the show, with the shovel being inserted downward vertically alongside the clam. Position yourself with one knee lower or on the sand so you can be ready for the next step.

4

You will have to experiment a little to find the best body position for you, but this is an excellent example to follow. The trick is to push the shovel handle downward (which will keep the clam from digging down deeper), while simultaneously inserting your hand behind the shovel. Good balance takes practice.

Razor Clams are generally closer to the surface in the surf. However, on days with heavy tidal surges they can be deeper. Continue moving your hand downward while adjusting your shovel upward. If you inserted your shovel in the perfect spot, your clam will be there. If not, feel around with your hand until you find your Razor Clam.

Clamming in the surf can be a real sport. This clammer is determined to get his Razor Clam and he has a lifetime of experience to help him get it. Battling waves is not for the faint of heart. If you're a novice, start in water less than six inches deep and always be aware of incoming waves. Complacency can be hazardous.

Pictured here is John Morris of Seaside, Oregon (known as "Johnny Mo" by locals). He is a Seaside native that has been Razor Clamming all his life. As you can see in the last few photos, Johnny Mo clearly knows what he is doing and he loves the sport of Razor Clamming. But most importantly, Johnny Mo always gets his Razor Clam!

Razor Clamming...

t's the end of a beautiful day, you're standing on the beach looking at one of the most stunningly beautiful sunsets in the world. The Pacific Northwest is generally known for rainy, cloudy days. Nevertheless, if you catch one beautiful sunset while out Razor Clamming, you will remember that moment for the rest of your life, and you'll be hooked.

Most evening tides are during the fall and winter months. If you're an avid Razor Clammer, knowing that roughly 40% of low tides during the year are at night, you will eventually get out there at that time. For the most part, the information in the "How to Dig Razor Clams" section on page 24 also applies to clamming in the evening. However, there are two issues worthy of

at Night

your attention when nighttime clamming.

1. Bring a quality light source. When there's a full moon it's surprising how long you can find shows after sunset. But moonlight varies nightly so come prepared with some type of lighting to help you see shows at night.

2. Beware of the rare sneaker wave – a wave that is much larger than the other waves around it – because if you're not paying attention they can sneak up on you with no warning.

I have been swimming, surfing and clamming the Pacific Ocean all of my life and only once have I been caught by a sneaker wave!

A more likely experience when clamming in or near the surf is getting so caught up in a dig that you don't notice an incoming wave. Even if it's not a sneaker wave, some waves are still big enough to knock you off balance. After years of clamming, I'm used to listening to waves and knowing what's coming at me just by the sound. But people do get knocked over by waves when they are not paying attention, so please be cautious while clamming in the surf.

Sneaker Waves

Few people I know have experienced a real sneaker wave. When I was 23, I took off for Seaside by myself for a nighttime clam tide. I used to do this a lot when I was broke, as crabbing, fishing and clamming were a source of food. That night I was clamming on wet sand when I noticed there was a long pause between waves. I didn't think much about it and kept wandering out further towards the ocean surf. After one very long pause, a large wave about four feet high hit me and completely knocked me over. Luckily I was wearing jeans because waders can fill with water pretty quickly. If you've ever wondered why your waders come with a belt, it's because it prohibits (or at least slows) them from filling with water.

Once a sneaker wave runs up the beach, it reverses course and flows back down into the ocean. This backwash is also a very strong force and can drag you out to the ocean. I was lucky that night and I was able to struggle up from the water to safety. To this day, I watch for calm periods, with large pauses between waves, as this is typically what happens prior to a sneaker wave.

When clamming at night, always be aware of the ocean conditions. If there are long pauses between waves and the surf seems to be receding, do not follow the surf out. And always wear your wader belt to slow them from filling with water.

Lighting Up the Beach

With all the lighting choices available today this seemingly simple purchase can quickly get complicated. However, keep in mind, as kids we would use any household flashlight we could find. For the last twenty years I've used the same Coleman twin-mantle lantern and I swear by it. With that said, there are some high-tech options that take lighting to a whole new level. Costs vary, but there is something to fit every need and budget.

Since there are so many options, you might want to consider fuel type and lantern style first. Other considerations when purchasing a light source include brightness, durability, water resistance and cost. For example, you can see on the Lantern Types chart, when you pay a premium for batteries, ease of use is great but there are other considerations, like battery performance in cold weather can affect the quality of the light.

There are pros and cons for all light types – LEDs, fuel, battery-operated, etc.–a little research will help you make the right choice for your clamming needs. For example, a headlamp frees you from carrying a lantern but the bright light can be bothersome when shined into the eyes of others. Some LED headlamps can't light up the beach as well as a lantern and, if they do, some create a glare that makes it harder to see the shows.

In your research, you will come across the word lumen(s), which is the standard unit of measure used to describe how well a light source will illuminate objects. Lumen ratings can sometimes be deceptive, often the lumen rating given on a product is based on raw lumens, which is not an accurate number because it doesn't take into account many things that will affect (aka, lower) the brightness of the light emitted. Use lumens as a general guide but also review the specifications on brightness, beam and distance. Lighting technology is evolving at a rapid pace and things are always changing.

Axt Family Lighting Preferences

My nephew Grant Howard uses a Coast HL8 LED Headlamp, which cost about $60. There are lower-priced headlamps, many $30 or less, and they all work to different degrees. Grant didn't just go by lumens when he made his choice and believes the brightness, adjustable beam and distance of this product is good for him. I've used it and the lighting is good, but my lantern is better (old habits die hard). Generally, Grant goes off clamming on his own but on occasion he will accidentally shine his headlamp in our eyes. That is a big downside to using a headlamp when clamming with others. However, he is our best clammer. Even on a tough night he gets his limit and we're happy to eat his clams so we tolerate the occasional flash in our eyes.

Uncle Gene Axt uses the Maglite 2-Cell D Flashlight. Experienced clammers will say, "A flashlight? That's a beginner's tool!" But they are relatively cheap, rugged, water resistant and they are very functional lights. It's also something many people already have in their house. A Maglite allows you to change the width of the

beam, effectively going from floodlight to spotlight, to get the best light at the correct distance. Gene clams on the wet sand only at night and it works well for him.

My son Nate and I use my old Coleman Twin-Mantle Lantern. Although carrying a lantern is more cumbersome than some other options, for lighting the beach to find shows it still does the best job. So why change? It works great and I won't use anything else even when alone. One of us is the spotter and the other does the digging. It takes a little longer for us to get our limits, but it's more fun for us doing it together. At night we like to clam in the wet sand, so the fact that lanterns aren't the best in the surf (bright headlamps are better) doesn't matter to us. So until we break something and can't find parts, why buy a new one? When we do buy a new one, it will most likely be the Coleman Northstar 2015, kind of spendy with street prices at $80 plus, but it's a great lantern and will last for a very long time.

Lighting technology continues to evolve and products are getting better all the time. Prices are dropping rapidly too. I'm continuing my search for the perfect LED headlamp built exclusively for Razor Clamming at night.

LIGHTING OPTIONS	Max Lumens	Avg High Runtime	Ruggedized Available	Water Resistance
Headlamp/LED	700	3 to 6 hrs.	Good	Good
Fuel Lantern	1700	5 to 30 hrs.	Fair	Fair
LED Lantern	1000	2 to 20 hrs.	Fair	Fair
Maglite	625	4 to 16 hrs.	Good	Good

LANTERN TYPES: PROS AND CONS	Fuel Cost	Availability	Manual Fuel Pump Effort	Cold Weather Effectiveness
Unleaded Gas	$	Best	Poor	Good
Kerosene	$$	Fair	Poor	Good
Coleman Fuel	$$$	Fair	Poor	Good
Propane	$$$$	Fair	Poor	Fair
Butane	$$$$	Poor	Good	Fair
Batteries	$$$$$	Good	Best	Poor

Should I Use a
Razor Clam Shovel or Gun?

Ultimately, the answer depends on your personal needs and long-term goals. Following are some considerations to keep in mind when deciding on which option is best for you.

Efficiency and Status

I've never seen a commercial Razor Clammer using a Razor Clam gun and for good reason. They only Razor Clam in the surf and they move fast. I've seen commercial Razor Clammers using their shovel like a Samurai sword master. Swinging their sword (clam shovel) swiftly into place, precisely next to the clam show. Descending into the sand at the exact depth — not too deep, nor too shallow — to get their hand on the clam, not wasting a nanosecond, prohibiting the Razor Clam from starting its decent downward deeper into the sand. Then, without standing up, a quick flick of the wrist and off into the clam bag it goes. I've seen them pull ten Razor Clams in just over a minute. Truly the sport of Razor Clamming at its finest and you can't do that with a gun in the surf.

For Beginners and Kids

It is faster and easier to learn how to Razor Clam with a gun so for beginners, and especially kids, it's just more fun to use a gun. It's also safer, because you don't have to use your hands to dig in the compacted wet sand. However, a gun doesn't work as well as a shovel in the surf. Because of this some will strongly disagree about starting with a gun, believing that if you are going to be clamming for a lifetime, it's best to master the shovel.

Breaking Razor Clam Shells

After going through all the effort, there is nothing worse than breaking a Razor Clam shell or cutting one in half. It's easy to do if you aren't careful; I've seen beginners with a bag full of broken Razor Clams. In my experience, it's easier to learn how to take a whole clam with a Razor Clam gun. Use a gun that is four to five inches in diameter and position it over the show, allowing a little more room on the ocean side, as Razor Clams dig down slightly towards the ocean. Pay close attention once the gun starts descending into the sand, listen and feel through the gun to make sure you don't hit the clam. If you do feel it, stop quickly and reposition the gun's downward decent to minimize breakage.

Mastering a Shovel

Some say that when you use a shovel you dig more with your hands to find the clam which reduces shell breakage. I think this is true in the surf's looser sand (one to eight inches underneath the water). But up in the denser wet sand, it's harder to move your hands around in the sand. Plus, figuring out which digging approach to use and how deep to dig prior to diving in with your hands, all add to the difficulty and time needed to master a shovel. This learning curve means more lost and broken clams.

Pulling Deep Razor Clams

A rougher surf causes Razor Clams to dig deeper into the sand, up to 3 feet deep. Shovel beginners often find themselves with their arm submerged in the sand, pulling the Razor Clam out by the tip of its neck! While the beginner was digging, the clam had time to lock its digger firmly into the sand and it is now holding on for dear life. If you let go of the neck, which is easy to do, you'll lose the clam! This scenario is caused by the clam's digger lock and the suction created from the sand surrounding the shell, which increases exponentially when you pull. This is worse than quicksand! There have even been university studies on using this Razor Clam suction technology for bridge and oil platform pillars.

Sometimes it can take a long time to slowly pull the clam out and all the while you are getting hit by waves. The war is on, it's you against the clam, "mono a mono"! Neither wanting to give up, the clam fighting for its life and you fighting for dinner!

When I was new at using a shovel, my bag would be full of Razor Clams with silly looking stretched-out necks (sometimes 6 inches or more) and I would be completely soaked from the constant waves. As a beginner these things can seem to defeat the benefits of using a shovel, but keep going until you become highly skilled at using a shovel, which takes time and practice!

Your Physical Condition

With Razor Clam guns you mostly use your back, but with shovels you use your back and knees. If you have knee problems, you are better served using a gun. If you're young and strong, the choice is yours. Either way, there is no wrong choice. Whichever method suits your physical needs, you'll be enjoying the day digging Razor Clams in no time!

WHEN TO USE A POUNDING STICK

Pounding sticks can be found at sporting goods stores. At the beach, you'll find sticks made specifically for Razor Clam pounding. A pounding stick will definitely increase your results, especially on days when shows just aren't showing!

In the Surf

The vast majority of Razor Clammers use a shovel in the surf, however there are people that like to use their gun in the surf, too. If you do, I highly recommend carrying something to pound the surf sand to find shows. A pounding stick or a long, thick walking stick with a blunt end will work. Keep in mind, this means you will be carrying two things: your gun and a pounding stick. To keep the surf from washing your pounding stick away when you're digging a clam, tie it to your waders. This feels cumbersome to me, so in the surf I like using a shovel and its butt end to pound for shows.

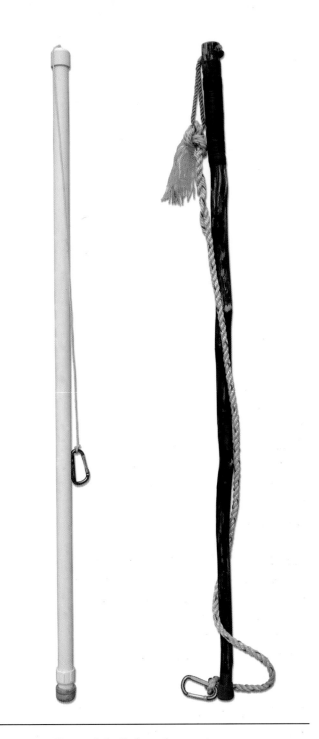

Pounding sticks help when using a gun.

On Wet Sand

If you use a gun, scan the beach for shows and when necessary stomp your feet or use your pounding stick to provoke shows. On wet sand, I like to carry a pounding stick. That way I'm prepared for whichever method seems to be working best on that particular day. Of course, if you are using a shovel, you only have to carry one thing as you can pound on the wet sand with the butt end of your shovel.

RAZOR CLAM GUN OPTIONS

There are many different types of Razor Clam guns so when finding the right gun for you the features to consider are length, weight, circumference, materials the gun is made of and cost. Many experienced Razor Clammers have serious opinions on what works best, but it's important to remember that they all get the job done. Recently, a new type of Razor Clam gun has entered the market. They are expensive, but they feature things like rubber-coated handles and special patented vacuum releases or relief tubes. If you can afford one, these guns will really minimize your digging effort. Whatever your needs, if you want to buy the correct gun the first time, here are the key considerations to evaluate:

Length: The longer the tube, the deeper a single plunge will go into the sand. To ease the stress on the back, you can find them up to 36 inches long. The majority are around 30", which is the size I've used for years. There are also junior sizes as short as 24 inches for kids, so everyone in the family can get in on the fun.

Weight: PVC and aluminum guns are the lightest, at around two pounds. Stainless-steel guns are considerably heavier at up to six pounds. For some, that extra weight feels like an unnecessary burden.

Circumference: Razor Clam guns can be found with 3-, 4- and 5-inch circumferences. The smaller the circumference, the more skill is required not to hit and/ or crack the clam. However, the larger the circumference, the more resistance you will get when pulling the gun up when it's full of sand. That is why guns with a five-inch circumference often have a T-handle extension (as seen in the five-inch-round metal guns on the next page).

T-Handle or Full-Length Tube: There are full-length and half-length (using a T-handle) guns. A longer tube minimizes the number of times you have to descend into the sand to get deep. It also increases the amount of sand and weight you are pulling up. Great for strong clammers or if you don't mind a bit of a work out for your dinner. However, most people that have 5-inch cylinders with a T-handle don't mind taking a couple of plunges when needed because the majority of the time you just need a single plunge.

Gun-cylinder circumference can minimize clam breakage significantly. However, the larger the circumference, the more sand and resistance when pulling up. On guns with a 5" circumference, they solved this weight problem by designing a T-handle which shortens the tube length, minimizing sand and resistance when pulling up.

Metal: Stainless-steel guns are arguably easier to plunge into the sand, they don't rust and are very durable. The down side is that they can weigh up to six pounds. Aluminum is light (around two pounds) and it doesn't rust, but it is more prone to corrosion. Remember, at the coast salt effects everything (other than stainless steel), and aluminum is more easily damaged by it.

Aluminum isn't as strong as stainless and forcing an aluminum gun down into the sand without rocking it back and forth a little can damage the gun. I have a nephew who is seriously strong and when starting out, bent two aluminum guns in this way. I use a painted aluminum gun which is still in good shape after seven years. It's lighter and descends just as easily as a stainless-steel gun (in my opinion).

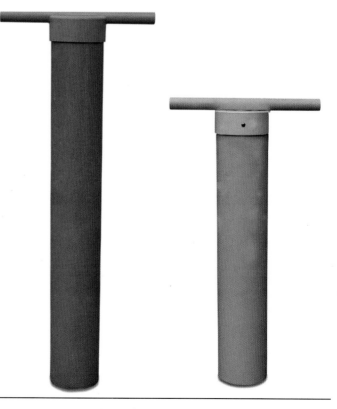

30" and 24" PVC guns.

Metal with Vacuum Release or Relief Tube: An additional metal tube (i.e., quarter inch or less in diameter) is welded to the outside of the gun's tube. After descending into the sand and putting your thumb on the gun's suction hole, the sand is sucked up with the gun. However, when pulling out of the sand, the additional vacuum or relief tube (which is always open), relieves the suction of all the external sand. So when pulling the gun out, you only have the weight of the sand and clam inside the tube. It's much easier on the back and a great idea!

PVC: The third most widely used synthetic plastic polymer in the world, PVC is a light option that is also inexpensive. However, the suction created around the plastic when pulling out of the sand feels very spongy compared to a metal gun. It is also harder to plunge into the sand, especially when you need to get deep, so you will need to plunge more often with a PVC gun. The major benefit of PVC is price. Great for people on a budget and it does get the job done.

Cost: At the time of this writing, PVC Razor Clam guns were found for as little as $7 and up to $30. Aluminum guns range between $50 and $70, and stainless-steel guns run up to $100. Specialty guns, with extras like a relief tube, are $100 plus!

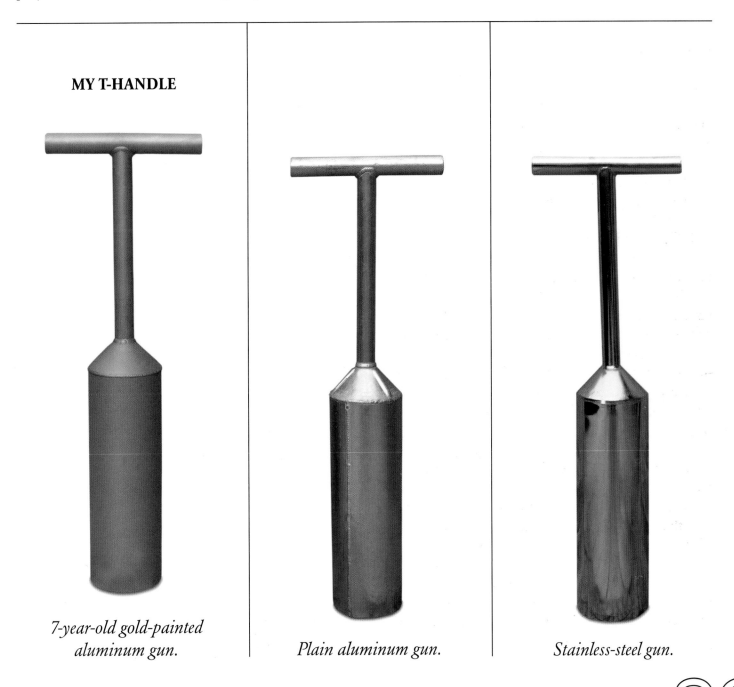

MY T-HANDLE

7-year-old gold-painted aluminum gun.

Plain aluminum gun.

Stainless-steel gun.

RAZOR CLAM SHOVEL OPTIONS

There are also numerous types of Razor Clam shovels but the main considerations when deciding which will work best for you are handle length, blade length, materials it's made from, weight and cost.

Handle Length: Handle lengths vary from 18" to 45". Short-handled shovels are much easier for kids to carry and use. However, some very good clammers like a short handle (with a long blade) because it's easier to maneuver while digging and easier to carry.

Longer handles fit the body of an adult better so you won't have to bend over as much when pounding for shows and digging for clams.

Specially Angled Shovel Blade and Lengths: Razor Clam shovels these days have 9" to 11" blades. In the past you could purchase shovels with up to 13" blades.

Short blades minimize the weight of the shovel. They also scoop less sand, which affects how much digging you have to do — so with a short blade there is less weight but you have to scoop more when the clams are deeper.

A longer blade can minimize your digging efforts. If you study the techniques in "How to Use a Razor Clam Shovel" on page 26, you will see the best way to dig a clam is to insert the blade vertically alongside the clam, then push the handle forward, which pushes the neck of the clam horizontally, making it harder for the razor clam to dig downward. Since a longer blade plunges deeper into the sand, you're more likely to reach the clam with your hand on the very first plunge. This is especially true if you are using a longer 13" blade, which gets your hand much deeper in the sand.

Into my 40's, my favorite shovel had a 26" handle and a 13" blade. Unfortunately, corrosion from the salt air destroyed it and I haven't seen a 13" blade on the market for many years. Some say that Razor Clams were more plentiful years ago and that there were more clams closer to the surface (in my recollection this is true) making a 13" blade more successful on a single plunge.

Metal: The majority of Razor Clam shovels are made of forged steel to keep the price down. Stainless steel is more expensive and heavier, but it will not rust and is very strong. Aluminum is light, but it's more prone to corrosion and much easier to damage when plunging

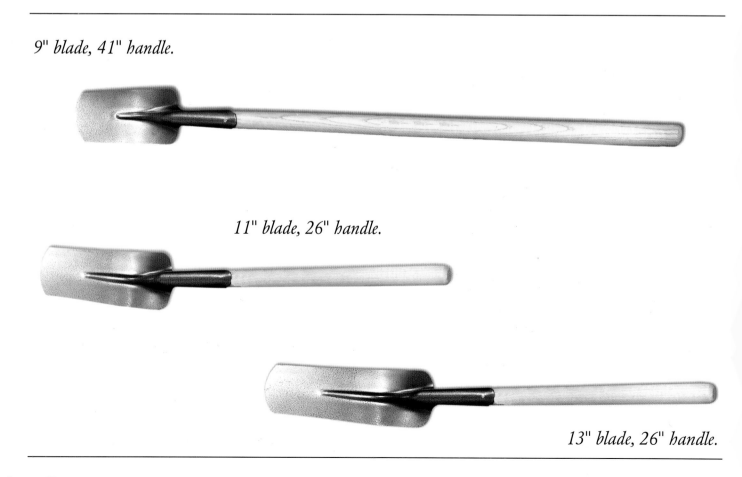

9" blade, 41" handle.

11" blade, 26" handle.

13" blade, 26" handle.

into the sand, consequently I don't see aluminum shovels being used anymore and they are very hard to find.

Weight: The lighter the shovel the easier it is to carry around, but I find a heavier shovel is better for pounding in the wet sand. There is less than a two-pound difference between a stainless-steel shovel and a forged-steel shovel. On a day when shows are hard to find, I stomp and pound like crazy, the extra weight hits the sand with more force so the little extra weight is worth it to me.

Cost: Forged-steel shovels cost $15 to $50, stainless-steel shovels are $75 plus.

WHAT WE USE
When taking kids and first-timers clamming, I hand out inexpensive PVC clam guns. You cannot bend or dent PVC easily, and if a gun gets lost it's not a big deal since PVC is cheap.

My Nephew Grant and my Uncle Gene will never be seen with a gun, anywhere, not even in their car. Same goes for a pounding stick. They are really good clammers and my uncle is a local, so they have a reputation to keep. Hence, Razor Clam shovel only!

My son Nate uses a gun on the wet sand and a shovel in the surf. He doesn't like carrying a pounding stick. He just stomps with his feet to find shows, if it is needed. That way he doesn't have to carry anything extra. It takes him a little longer to limit out and he doesn't care, he just loves being on the beach for as long as he can.

Over the years I continue to adjust my technique and change the equipment I use. Today, in the surf I use a shovel. I have a 41" handle and a short 9" stainless-steel blade. When pounding the surf for shows, the long handle makes it much easier on my back. The extra weight from the stainless steel is more effective when pounding on the wet sand, as well.

When I'm on the wet sand, which I am more often these days, I use a painted aluminum, 5" circumference tube with a T-handle. On the wet sand a gun is just easier on my knees and aluminum is light (stainless-steel guns are too heavy for me). I've had mine for seven years, without any sign of corrosion. I also carry a pounding stick tied to my waders when the tidal surge is rougher because clam shows are harder to find, that way I can pound and stomp like crazy.

Razor Clamming
Clothing

Razor Clamming is one of the few inexpensive family activities left. Even fishing license fees can get very expensive in comparison to the cost of a shellfish license in Oregon and Washington. Inexperienced Razor Clammers often just wear tennis shoes and jeans, add a PVC Razor Clam gun and a bag to carry the clams and you have an inexpensive pastime the whole family can enjoy.

On a beautiful summer's day, even some experienced Razor Clammers find it hard to resist cutoffs and tennis shoes. I highly discourage going barefoot as Razor Clam shells can be sharp and the occasional piece of glass can ruin family's day quickly. The photo here shows the various clothing that can be worn when clamming, (left to right) I'm wearing chest waders with surf shoes, my son, Nate, has a pair of kids' plastic waist waders, Uncle Gene is in cutoffs and tennis shoes and Uncle Bob just couldn't resist going barefoot on a beautiful day (which I don't recommend).

Even if you only take your family on an outing once or twice a year, you can see that you don't need much to get started. Waders are really nice but if it's hard to justify the cost, don't let that get in your way. When clamming, you'll find people dressed in every way imaginable. Once you decide you'll be clamming for years to come, it's much easier to justify the garb and it's well worth the expense.

So keep in mind:
- ✓ You can limit out in tennis shoes.
- ✓ Rubber boots are inexpensive and better than tennis shoes.
- ✓ Hip waders cost a little more, but are much better than rubber boots.
- ✓ Waist waders are better than hip waders but, again, a little more money.
- ✓ Chest waders are so much better than hip or waist waders, if you can afford them they're the best way to go!

I'm in chest waders, Nate in waist waders, Uncle Gene in tennis shoes, Uncle Bob in bare feet (which I don't recommend)

FOR SERIOUS CLAMMERS

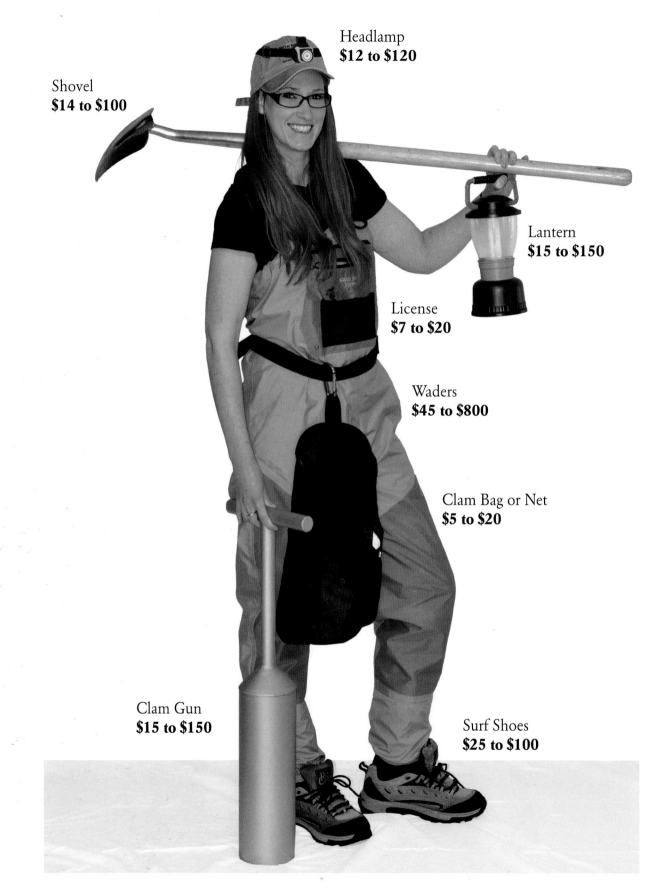

Headlamp
$12 to $120

Shovel
$14 to $100

Lantern
$15 to $150

License
$7 to $20

Waders
$45 to $800

Clam Bag or Net
$5 to $20

Clam Gun
$15 to $150

Surf Shoes
$25 to $100

If you get serious about clamming, appropriate clothing becomes a necessity. For example, on a winter's nighttime Razor Clam outing, you'll want to be well prepared to be both safe and comfortable.

Kate Reeg, on the left, models some clamming apparel. There are inexpensive options for each item and, of course, some can get very expensive depending on the item's durability, performance, style, and prestige. Chest waders are a good example. You can find a pair for around $45. If you're looking for the top of the line, you'll pay around $800. And there are many options in between,

Clamming garb is easy to find, most sporting goods stores in major cities will have what you need.

Taking the Angst Out of Choosing Waders

Being wet and cold or hot and sweaty can make you a very unhappy clammer. Years ago, there were not many wader options. In the 1960's, my grandfather used rubber hip waders, which for the time worked well.

Into my thirties, I just wore jeans and brought along an extra pair to change into when I was done clamming. Sometimes I froze my hiney off and would cut the day short because I was just too miserable to continue. I remember it was very painful to pay for my first pair of waders. Of course, if I only knew then, what I know now! Waders are so worth the expense and I should have bought a pair years before I did! Learn from my mistake and buy the right pair of waders first, you'll be much more comfortable and save money in the long run.

Over the past few decades, waders have improved a lot. Go to the internet for detailed technical information on materials, seaming, breathability, temperature, humidity, durability, longevity, comfort, sizes and prices…there are so many manufacturers and styles you can fall into wader abyss. To save you some time, I will share my experiences with waders, and list key issues to be aware of when purchasing a new pair. I'll provide a few of the manufactures that I'm familiar with, but remember there are many options and all I can say with confidence is buy a pair of waders, you'll be glad you did!

Waders I've Tried

The first pair of waders I purchased in the early 80's were made of a rubber material (today, PVC, rubber and vinyl materials share similar traits). They were waist high, and had booties so I could slip them into my tennis shoes. They were cheap and I was so happy! I started to limit out more often too, mostly because I was able to spend more time in the surf. Eventually, I discovered a few problems with this rubber material. When it was cold, they kept you dry but not warm. Since rubber doesn't breathe, my jeans would become wet with sweat and it would get very damp and cold inside my waders. In the summer, my body was trapped in a sauna making it very hot and sweaty! I couldn't afford anything more, and they were much better than nothing. The same holds true today!

In the mid 80's, I finally decided to plop down some big bucks (for me anyway) and buy a pair of 5mm neoprene chest waders. It was a huge improvement in my comfort. When it was cold, the insulating properties of neoprene kept me warm. They don't breathe well so when it was warm and I would sweat it would become damp inside. They were very durable and wore very well. Neoprene waders were a major improvement over rubber.

In the mid 90's, I purchased new neoprene waders for my wife and I, this time in the thinner 3.5mm. They felt lighter and were a little more comfortable. They were supposed to be cooler in the summer but I felt just as hot as I did in the 5mm neoprene. Today you can get 2mm neoprene waders but I've never tried them. I still have a pair of neoprene waders and occasionally, if it's really cold, I'll still wear them.

In 2001, I bought my first pair of waders made from breathable, waterproof fabric. What an improvement! For me, it was the biggest improvement to waders ever made. I didn't realize that what you wear underneath the waders determines how breathable they will be. Wear jeans and they will still get sweaty and damp, but it's much better than it was with previous materials. You need to wear breathable underwear to really get the benefits of wicking sweat away from your body. That holds true today with all of the new fabrics. Once I figured that out, I finally found a truly awesome wader for clamming!

Throughout the 2000's, I have purchased Joe Outdoors, Frogg Toggs, Caddis, and Cabela's waders, all using waterproof, breathable fabrics. I've had great experiences with them all. I will say, that the many sizes available from Caddis have made them my favorite pair, since I'm stout and some manufacturers have limited size options. Each manufacturer has different features that make their products stand out in one category or another.

WHAT TO CONSIDER WHEN BUYING WADERS

Style: Hip waders, waist waders or chest waders – for bay clamming they all work well. For Razor Clamming I strongly recommend chest waders, and not just for clamming in the surf. If you want to go out on the sand bars, chest waders are the only way to stay dry. Buy a pair with a belt and you can fold the chest down when bay clamming.

Belts: A belt is a very important safety option. The primary use for the belt is to slow the water from filling up your waders if you become submerged. On hot days, you can fold the chest part of your waders down and the belt will keep your pants up. You can fasten your clamming bag to your belt; the loops come in handy, too.

Stocking-Foot or Boot-Foot: Boot-foot waders have permanently attached boots so you don't have to buy boots or worry about losing them. I've always used stocking-foot waders because the boots on the boot-style waders never fit my feet properly. With the stocking-foot style, I can use any shoe (even old tennis shoes) and size I want. If you can spring for a nice pair of stocking-foot wader boots, they slip on easier, keep the sand out of your boots, have better ankle support and are more comfortable. For clamming, make sure you get rubber-soled wader boots, not felt-soled.

Wader Materials: Hot, cold, rainy, sunny, windy, wet, stormy – and sometimes all of these conditions in a single day. Welcome to the Pacific Northwest coast! Buy the right material and you will be comfortable no matter what the weather is like. Here are some considerations when selecting wader materials and fabrics.

Rubber Waders: Heavier, stiffer, not breathable and less comfortable. Chest waders work best in the surf, but I only see waist and hip waders made of this material these days. Commercial clammers wear rubber coats and pants because they like the durability and affordability of rubber. For me, comfort in a chest wader is required so I don't recommend rubber waders for Razor Clamming anymore.

Nylon and PVC Waders: These materials are not breathable and will trap sweat inside the wader, making you damp and uncomfortable. I do not recommend these materials either, although they are cheap and

kids' sizes can be found for as little as $12. For the first-timer and kids, these waders will work and are definitely better than nothing.

Neoprene Waders: For years neoprene has dominated the market. They are water proof, very durable and come in 5mm, 3mm and 2mm thicknesses. It's tough to beat neoprene when it gets really cold outside but they are not breathable and will trap your sweat inside. You'll find many clammers on the beach with neoprene waders and they work and wear very well.

Breathable Materials (like GORE-TEX): Lightweight, breathable, water proof and comfortable. They even breathe when submerged under water. You do have to wear a base layer of breathable underwear to allow them to work effectively. Goodbye to sweat being trapped in your waders. Because of this important benefit these new fabrics are replacing neoprene waders. Available in lightweight and up to heavier 4-layer materials for really cold days. In the Northwest, I'm most comfortable in the lightweight materials, even when it is cold. If you can afford it, I see no reason to buy anything but breathable, waterproof chest waders for Razor Clamming.

Price: Rubber, Nylon and PVC are the least expensive. If that is all you can afford or you're just starting out, they work. There are neoprene and breathable waders on the market today for less than $100 that work well, too. You pay more for increased durability, performance and comfort. Once you get over $300 there are differing opinions on value and I've seen them up to $800. Someday, I gotta get me a pair of those (in my dreams)!

Size: When your waders are too small it makes it hard to bend over to dig your clam, too big and you feel like the Goodyear Blimp. Not all manufacturers offer short or stout sizes, or they might offer stout but only in an extra-large. Take your height, inseam, chest, max girth and foot measurements before you head off to the store. Plan to try on different sizes while there. If they don't have your size, many times they can order it and deliver the waders to your home. For really hard to find sizes, most online stores have good return policies these days. Don't settle for waders that don't fit right, your size is out there.

Is Razor Clamming a Sport or Hobby?

This topic can be controversial. I didn't give it much thought until Long Beach, Washington started giving prize money for the largest and best-looking Razor Clam limit. When I thought about it a little more I realized in our group clamming is always a competition! On good days, you might be the only one to get a limit and on a bad day the only one to get a single clam. Nobody wants to be "that guy".

I looked up the definition of "sport" and it says:

"An activity involving physical exertion and skill in which an individual or team competes against another or others for entertainment."

- **Does Razor Clamming require physical exertion? Sometimes.**
- **Does Razor Clamming require skill? Sometimes.**
- **Do Razor Clammers compete? Sometimes.**

I will never forget one day in the mid 90's when John Morris, Gene Axt, my dad Ken Axt, Sr. and I all went clamming in Gearhart, Oregon during a really rough storm. That day my dad refused to get out of the car, it was too rough and rainy! Finding a show in the cold, sideways rain and raging pounding surf definitely took skill. And when you found one, digging it up while waist-high waves crashed into you took both skill and physical exertion. We kept looking at each other's bags in keen competition, nobody wanted to be the one to not get his limit. I got rolled in the surf that day, I was soaking wet but still didn't give up! When the tide was coming in, we counted the day's results. I had one Razor Clam (I still hate admitting that), Gene had three and Johnny Mo had nine. Twenty years ago and I still remember the clam count.

I enjoy watching the skill, physical exertion and competitiveness of commercial Razor Clammers as much today as I did when I was a boy. Each commercial Razor Clammer has different clothing and tools. Each pounds the sand with a specific rhythm and reach. Each has a slightly different set-up, stance and position, as they bend and kneel with artful skill that pushes their body's abilities. With unique surgical skill, they plunge their shovel into the surf's underwater sand alongside a disappearing show. All to allow for a single dive of the hand, quick retrieval of the clam and, with a flick of the wrist, a toss into their huge Razor Clam net. Then on to the next clam in rapid succession, moving the shovel swiftly with the art and rhythm of a Samurai.

- **Physical exertion? Absolutely!**
- **Skill? No Question!**
- **Competition? Absolutely!**

I started Razor Clamming around 8 years old. Although I went many times, one particular day stands out. It was the perfect sunny, spring day, with not a cloud in the sky. The tidal surge was extremely low and it seemed like the ocean runoff took forever to run back into the sea. Perfect for a Razor Clam feeding frenzy! We didn't even have to look for shows, we just went from one necking clam to another. If you didn't see one squirting at you, it was only a few minutes before you could see the "V" in the ocean runoff. The clams were so close to the surface, we could dig some of them out with just our hands.

- **Physical exertion? Not for us!**
- **Skill? It was the first time for some of us!**
- **Competition? Just a bunch of young boys having fun!**

In my opinion it's a great Sport and Hobby. As long as your out there participating you'll be a "Happy Clammer"!

BELL BUOY OF SEASIDE

The Bell Buoy Fish Market in Seaside, Oregon has been harvesting and selling Razor Clams for over 57 years. They supply the majority of Razor Clams to all Oregonians. They have trained and managed many commercial Razor Clammers. Next time you're in Seaside stop and ask them what they think? Sport or hobby? The debate continues!

DENNIS COMPANY RAZOR CLAM COMPETITION

Want to compete? Thanks to the Dennis Company and Washington Department of Fish and Wildlife you can compete for biggest clam and best-looking limit in Long Beach, Washington every April. It is judged by the Washington Department of Fish & Wildlife. Get up early and be ready to go toe to toe with some of the best Razor Clammers on the Oregon and Washington coasts.

WHAT THE BEST CLAMMERS WON'T TELL YOU

Razor Clamming Strategy: The tide, moon, weather, water temperature, El Niño, a calm surf (lower wave swells or tidal surges) and other factors help you decide the best time to get your limit. The pros know how to find and correlate the tidal surge data that marine captains and surfers use. Experts know how high, how low, the time in-between waves and how rough the surf swells will ultimately be. All to determine at what times the razor clams will be feeding most heavily. As they say, "When the surfs up, the clamming is down."

Razor Clam Tactics: Shifting sand dunes under the surf's intertidal zone provide safe haven for Razor Clam larvae that wash up against and lodge themselves in the sand. Since shifting sands change yearly, experts frequent the beach gathering this information to find the best spots and, more specifically, the best sandbar spots. Of course, you have to be a lifetime friend of a local for them to share this valuable information with you. Even then, some just don't share!

Water temperatures can vary north to south. Razor Clams prefer cooler water temperatures, but when it reaches 55 degrees or over their reproductive cycle starts and their feeding slows down. Since water temperatures vary frequently and sometimes in short distances, clamming can be better just a short distance down the beach where the water is cooler.

Cleaning your
Razor Clams

I have been cleaning clams for fifty years and it is sad to see how much misinformation there is on the internet, especially in videos. With that said, cleaning Razor Clams can be easily explained with just a few instructional photos. I've broken it down into steps. If you have a lot of clams to clean, I recommend you split the tasks into three stations: Deshelling, cutting, and washing. A team effort can really speed things up!

PROPERLY CLEANED RAZOR CLAMS

- The "digger" and "neck" are not separated, the entire clam is in one piece.
- The "windows" (after the clam is butterflied, the translucent membrane on both sides) have no nicks, holes or punctures.
- The gills and palps (see photos) are both completely removed.
- Most clams have a "crystalline style". This clear, thin, inch-long rod is good for the clam's digestion. It is edible, but usually removed.

- The intestine that runs through the digger is removed but many people think the digger foot membrane is the best part of the clam – do not wash (or scrub) out this fleshy membrane.

Finally, you can use anything to clean a clam, however the proper tools can make the job so much easier. Many professionals just use a sharp knife for the entire process and they're doing 300 or more clams a day. I like my fingers and it's easy to cut yourself with a very sharp knife so I use scissors with very thin blades and sharp-pointed tips (regular kitchen scissors are larger, see photos). These scissors make it easy to slip into the syphon holes and quickly maneuver around the clam.

I've seen many different techniques and what follows is the process I learned from Razor Clam cleaners at the Crab Broiler in Seaside, Oregon back in the 1960's. Today, all restaurants and seafood stores worth their weight use this technique.

CLEANING RAZOR CLAMS

1

Shelling the Clam
Dunk the clam in boiling water and wait a few seconds for the shell to pop open. Remove them from the water immediately. If you use a netted clamming bag, you can do many clams in one dunk.

2

Cool the Meat
It is important not to cook the clam in the boiling water, so dunk them in cold water right after removing them from the boiling water. This stops them from cooking. When they're cold, they're ready for cleaning.

3

Cut Siphon Tip
At the top of the neck, snip the dark part off the tip. This will make the two siphon holes a little larger to easily fit your scissors into.

4

Open the Body
Starting at the first siphon hole, insert the scissors tip and cut open. Then cut the second siphon hole and continue down the body's zipper, this will open the entire clam. When butterflied, the two sides are referred to as windows, be careful not to cut or nick the windows.

5

Gills and Mouth
Next cut the right gill and palp (the clam's mouth), flip the digger over and trim the left gill and remaining palp. Again, be careful not to nick the windows while trimming.

6

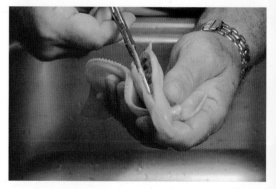

Open the Digger
Hold the clam so that you can slip the scissors into the clam's digger bottom and snip it open deeply enough to butterfly. It should lay flat when done. Remove the intestines but not the membrane (fleshy part of the digger foot), which is tender and great eating.

7

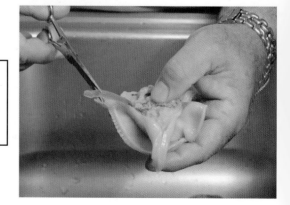

Remove Clear Rod
Most clams have a clear rod, the crystalline style. The rod is edible, but discard.

8

Cut Stomach Out

Make a cut around the stomach, cutting as much of it as possible without damaging any membrane. The more precise the cut, the easier it will be to wash out what's left.

9

Wash Stomach

Open the clam; from behind, push the stomach out with your thumb (this is more difficult if not cut precisely). Wash the neck and stomach with clean water. Remove all the brown and dark-colored residue.

10

Wash Digger

Do the same process for the digger (or foot). Do not wash out the fleshy part of the digger. For some, this part is a delicacy and the best eating of the clam. Just be sure to remove all the green and brown residue.

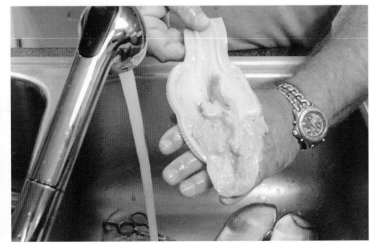

11

Perfect End Result

Front side of the clam with the neck and digger intact. No nicks or damage to the clam's windows. Neck, body and digger are all open to create a (steak like) flat Razor Clam for cooking.

Storing Razor Clams

When we purchase shellfish from grocery stores we treat them as we treat all edible sea creatures – the sooner you eat it the better! If it smells bad, remember the addage "When in doubt, throw it out!" Spoiled fish can make you sick and in extreme cases can even be fatal. These same rules apply to Razor Clams.

Most clams can stay alive in their shells for days, as long as they have ample oxygen and are kept cool – ideally between 34° and 38° Fahrenheit – and moist. Razor Clam shells don't close all the way like most bay clams, such as steamers, so they will dry out quicker. They also have a much higher percentage of meat to protective shell, so they are more susceptible to temperature changes and need more oxygen so it is imperative that you store them properly to keep them alive. The good news is you don't have to clean your Razor Clams immediately. But once a razor clam dies, you have to throw it out. For this reason, even if I store the clams properly, I always clean, refrigerate or freeze them by the next day, preferably the same day. Any Razor Clam connoisseur will tell you that nothing tastes better than a Razor Clam caught, cleaned and cooked on the same day.

HOW NOT TO KILL YOUR RAZOR CLAMS

When touched Razor Clams should withdraw their siphon and tighten their shell to minimize exposure to the elements. If the neck is hanging all the way out of the shell and it stays limp when touched, it could be dead. Move it around and spray a little water on it to get it to move, even slightly, but if it doesn't move and has been out of its environment too long it is probably dead. Here are some ways I see people shortening the life of their Razor Clams.

Leaving Them in A Bucket of Water: Razor Clams need oxygen to survive. Once they suck the oxygen out of the water they're in, they will suffocate. The temperature of the water, what kind of water, the ratio of clams to available water are all factors that determine how long they will survive. Because of all these different factors, it's hard to know exactly how long your clams will live in water. I can tell you, it isn't ever necessary to purge Razor Clams submerged in water, since you should be cleaning them within 48 hours anyway.

Covering Them With Ice in A Cooler: If you pour ice over your clams they can get too cold and even freeze to death. As the ice melts, filling your cooler with water, the clams on the bottom can suffocate. Putting the lid on the cooler will limit the amount of oxygen available to them. All of these mistakes make for unhappy clams.

Leaving Them Uncovered or in a Sealed Container in the Refrigerator: Uncovered, the fan in the refrigerator circulates the air, reducing the moisture in the air, which will dry out your clams. A tightly sealed container will shut off the oxygen supply and suffocate your clams.

KEEPING YOUR RAZOR CLAMS ALIVE

Now that you understand what your clams don't like,

here's how to keep them fresh. While digging clams use an inexpensive clamming bag made from nylon mesh or another material (like burlap) that breathes. You can also wash your clams off in the ocean while they are in this kind of bag, which is very convenient.

For the trip home, put a towel in the bottom of your cooler, set your ice in bags around your clams and leave the lid cracked open to allow oxygen in. If your clams start to dry out, put a wet towel over them.

I try to clean my clams the same day I catch them but often that just isn't convenient. I keep them refrigerated in a large strainer (or burlap bag when I have a lot of clams) with a dry towel underneath and a wet towel on top. I periodically check to see if they need more moisture and, if so, add water to the towel as needed. By following these simple steps, you'll be surprised how long your clams can stay alive.

REFRIGERATING AND FREEZING CLEANED RAZOR CLAMS

Surprisingly, once cleaned, Razor Clam meat has a pretty long shelf life. While it's refrigerated, water from the clam's meat will drain out and this changes the texture and taste of the clam, so the less time in the refrigerator the better. Freeze what you are not going to eat as quickly as possible. For the best quality, I use my refrigerated cleaned clams within 2 to 4 days.

After they've been cleaned Razor Clams freeze really well. The best way is with a vacuum-sealed bag with just a little bit of water. Let the clams freeze for 15 minutes in the vacuum bag before you seal it. That way, you can vacuum more air out of the bag and get a tighter seal. Heavy-duty freezer bags work great, too. Just squeeze as much air out of the bag as you can.

When Razor Clams are packaged and frozen, the water in their flesh expands. When thawed, the water shrinks and drains, making the meat's texture less dense. As with all seafood, with time in your freezer, the flavor and color will change too. For this reason, some people add a little salt to the water before freezing. My grandmother always added a 50/50 mix of milk and water then froze it all in milk cartons. Many fish-processing plants today use a brine (mix of salt and water) prior to freezing. Since the freezing point can change when using additives (for example, salt water requires lower temperatures to freeze), mixing additives incorrectly could do more harm than good. Fish-processing plants freeze at -4°F and lower to kill any parasites that may be present. Home freezers are usually between 10°F and 0°F. Just remember, if you use additives you need to know your new freeze point and how cold your freezer can get.

I've used all of these methods and now I usually add a little tap water, or nothing at all when there is enough clam juice in the bag. More important than additives is a thermostat and making sure your freezer is at 0°F or lower (most newer freezers can get to 0°F). I prefer to use heavy-duty freezer bags or vacuum-sealed freezer bags, additives aren't worth the trouble. For the best quality, I freeze at 0°F or lower and eat the clams within 6 months.

Razor Clam

Recipes

Razor Clams were a very popular item on the menu at the Crab Broiler Restaurant in Seaside. They would clean the clams, give them a wash in milk and beaten eggs, bread them and freeze them, all at the same time. I've done this and it works pretty well. For a quick and delicious dinner, just pull a bag from the freezer and fry them up. When freezing there is a chemical reaction with the breading and clam that makes the breading stick to the clam better.

Most people in the Pacific Northwest prefer to bread and fry their Razor Clams. There are countless variations on this simple cooking method. Just consider the numerous oils you can use for frying (olive, canola, sesame, peanut, etc.) and frying pans (cast iron, steel, non-stick, deep-fryer, etc.), washes (egg, milk, buttermilk, etc.) and finally, breading (flour, panko, cracker meal, ground butter crackers, etc.). The variations are endless, and all are delicious!

Of course, I feel my family had the best recipe. When my grandmother passed away, it was my turn to keep the family tradition going. For 20 years, all I ever heard was, "These aren't as good as grandma's!" Then, I had a dream. I was a young boy, standing in the kitchen watching grandma frying clams. I saw her scooping bacon fat out of a coffee can. Finally, I remembered her trick and now I'm passing the tradition on to my son and nephew!

For the beginner, here is a very easy recipe to follow. There are really only two issues you need to focus on: First, getting your clams brown without overcooking them, which will make them tough and chewy. Second, making sure the breading doesn't fall off while frying, which makes the presentation unappealing.

The reason people overcook clams is because it takes too long to brown them. A common mistake is using an oil like Extra Virgin Olive Oil. It has a very low smoke point (325 degrees) so it takes too much time to brown your clam, and by then it's like shoe leather. Corn, canola and vegetable oil are readily available and all have higher smoke points (450 and 400 degrees respectively). With these oils your Razor Clams will brown faster and won't be as overcooked and tough. A minute on each side is only a guideline. You want your Razor Clam to be nicely browned and not so tough that you can't cut it with a fork. At the same time, you don't want it undercooked, limp and still raw.

For breading, we use an egg and milk wash then flour. There is a simple trick to make sure your coating sticks to the clam. After they are nicely floured, don't immediately drop them in the frying pan. If you let them rest for at least 15 minutes, the flour adheres to the clam better. Usually, I prep all my clams prior to guests coming over by putting them on baking sheets lined with wax paper and refrigerating them.

Fried Razor Clams

INGREDIENTS

1 pound Razor Clams
3 eggs mixed with
1/4 cup milk

2 cups flour
1/4-inch-deep corn,
vegetable or canola oil

Salt to taste
Lemon slices
Tartar sauce

1. Mix eggs and milk.
2. Drain clams well to ensure the egg wash and flour adhere to them. Dunk them in the wash and then into the flour to coat them.
3. Once floured, lay clams on aluminum foil or wax paper and let rest for fifteen minutes or more so the coating will adhere to clam better.
4. Season with salt while resting (then other side while in the frying pan).
5. Add about 1/4 inch of oil to pan, heat on medium (not high) close to the oils smoke point.
6. Test the oil by dipping the end of a clam in the oil, if it doesn't start to fry immediately, it's not hot enough. If you burn the oil, don't use it, start over.
7. Cook clams until brown, about 1 minute on each side. Make sure clams are not limp (too raw) or too stiff (tough). To keep oil hot, don't add too many clams in a single pan.
8. Serve with lemon wedges and/or tartar sauce.

I've eaten Po Boy sandwiches in New Orleans, New York, Portland (Maine) and Boston, where they use everything from fried oysters, shrimp and lobster, but I still haven't seen a Northwest restaurant offer up a Razor Clam Po Boy. I started eating my grandmother's Razor Clams in Seaside, Oregon in 1964 and to this day, there is only one thing as good and that's a **Razor Clam Poor Boy**.

Razor Clam Poor Boy

Razor Clams, 4 to 8 – enough for four sandwiches. Fried, follow the recipe on page 55 or use leftovers.

Miso Mayonnaise
1/2 cup mayonnaise
2 teaspoons white or red miso
1 teaspoon Dijon mustard
1 squeeze fresh lime juice
Optional: Sriracha sauce
to taste

In a small bowl, add the mayonnaise, miso and lime juice and mix until smooth. Season to taste. If you prefer a little heat, add some Sriracha. Miso is very salty, but I add two tablespoons. Keep Miso Mayonnaise covered in refrigerator and it will last as long as plain mayonnaise.

Four French Sandwich Rolls
Preheat the oven to a low broil. Butter the rolls and place on a baking sheet. Broil until golden, 2 to 3 minutes, remove from oven and let sit. You want your rolls crisp, even after adding the cole slaw.

Assembling the Sandwich
Liberally spread Miso Mayonnaise on both sides of the rolls. Add the Razor Clams and cole slaw. Serve immediately.

Cole Slaw
4 cups chopped cabbage (about 1/2 head)
1/8 cup diced carrots
2 tablespoons minced onions
1/2 teaspoon salt
1/8 teaspoon pepper
1/2 cup mayonnaise
1/4 cup sweet Asian vinegar

Chop and dice cabbage and carrots, add to large bowl and stir in minced onions. In a separate bowl, add spices, mayo and vinegar and mix until smooth and creamy. Pour sauce over the vegetables and mix thoroughly. Cover bowl and refrigerate several hours or overnight before serving. Make sure the sauce is not too thin, you don't want your cole slaw to soak the bun, so a drier slaw (thicker dressing) is best.

Fried Razors with Sautéed Mushrooms, Caramelized Onions and Cole Slaw

INGREDIENTS

15 fried Razors from previous recipe
2 large onions, sliced
1 clove garlic, chopped
4 cups mushrooms, sliced
¼ cup butter (one cube)
Salt (to taste
Freshly ground black pepper (to taste)
1 tablespoon granulated sugar
2 lemons, cut into wedges

1. Prepare fried Razor Clams from previous recipe and set aside.
2. Melt butter in 12" skillet over medium high to high heat. Add garlic, mushrooms, onions, salt and pepper. Cook, stirring frequently until tender, about 8-10 minutes.
3. To caramelize add sugar and continue to cook until browned.
4. Place fried Razors on plate and spoon sautéed mushrooms and caramelized onions over the top.

Favorite Cole Slaw

3/4 cup mayonnaise
1/2 cup buttermilk
1/4 cup milk
3/4 cup sugar
3 tablespoons lemon juice

3 tablespoons white vinegar
6 cups cabbage, finely chopped
1/2 cup finely chopped carrots
2 tablespoons minced onion

1. Chop carrots and cabbage into very small pieces.
2. In a separate bowl mix all other ingredients until sauce is smooth.
3. Combine sauce with cabbage, carrots and onion, mix well.
4. Refrigerate one hour to overnight.
5. Serve with Razor Clams, lemon wedges and cole slaw.

Bay Clams

When I was twelve and living in Portland, I had a neighbor friend whose dad was a Marine Biologist. One summer day, my friend asked if I wanted to join him and his dad for a quick trip to the coast to harvest some mussels. I had no clue what a mussel was but it sounded like fun. A few hours later, we were on the beach in Pacific City, prying mussels off the rocks at low tide. We were back in Portland in time for dinner with buckets full of mussels.

It amazes me how many native Northwesterners are unaware of the plethora of free seafood available up and down the Oregon and Washington coasts, including Washington's Puget Sound area which has literally hundreds of areas to clam. With a garden shovel (or rake) and a bucket, you're ready to harvest bay clams. It's a great activity for the entire family, it's low cost and super easy to do. And what is better than being at the Pacific Coast or beautiful Puget Sound?

For those of you that spend a fortune on organic foods at pricey organic food stores, there is a place I like to call "nature's own seafood department" where you can get shellfish for free, as wild, fresh and natural as it gets, located a short distance down the highway at your nearest beach, bay or estuary. Some, like oysters, are just lying there and all you have to do is pick them up. Other shellfish, like cockles, are just inches below the surface and take very little effort to dig. Some can be huge (i.e., geoduck clams average 2 pounds) and require some skill and effort. But all are free for the taking – wild, all-natural clams, oysters and mussels. A healthy choice without spending your whole paycheck!

Ken Axt at Netarts Bay, on the Oregon Coast

FOUR REASONS CLAMS ARE GOOD FOR YOU:

1. Clams Are High in Protein and Low in Calories: Even higher than other types of shellfish, such as scallops and oysters. High-quality lean protein is great for your weight because it can make you feel fuller longer. It's also good if you are at risk for cardiovascular disease or type 2 diabetes.

2. Clams Are High in Omega-3: Low in saturated fat and high in omega-three fatty acids, helps lower blood pressure, reduce triglycerides and decrease plaque, which, according to the experts, all reduce heart attacks and strokes.

3. Clams Are High in Vitamin B-12: Clams are high in A, B and C vitamins. This includes B1, B2, B3 and B12. They are one of the best sources of B-12 available, which promotes healthy hair and stimulates your metabolism.

4. Clams Are High in Iron: Most of us know shellfish are a good source of minerals such as zinc, selenium and magnesium. But, ounce for ounce, clams are higher in iron than beef or liver.

There are so many great ways to make low-calorie dishes with clams: You can steam, bake, barbecue, sauté in white or red wine and they go with vegetables such as tomatoes, lemongrass, cilantro, celery, mushrooms and so many others!

I like eating all-natural foods, but cage-free, range-free and wild meats are often too expensive. However, I can harvest clams inexpensively and easily in fairly close proximity to every major city in Oregon and Washington.

I often ponder how harvesting Bay Clams has not changed for so many years. Lewis and Clark did the same thing I do today (in their journals they mention eating "little round clams") and what the Pacific Northwest Indian Tribes did hundreds of years earlier.

BEST PLACES TO GO BAY CLAMMING
Oregon's Unbelievable Coastline

I'm a native Oregonian and like many Oregonians I love the beauty of this state. I've been to almost every state in the U.S. and each has its unique qualities but none come close to the Oregon experience. A fairly low population with mountains, rivers, lakes, bays, natural forests, and the ocean. I think all Oregonians have an inner sense of Oregon's nature. No matter where I lived or visited, there was always a vibration in my soul that was just a little off tune, which only Oregon's nature can cure!

There are twelve notable Oregon bays that, at

the right tides, offer good potential to limit out on a variety of clams and mussels in a reasonable time. In Oregon, oysters are only legal for commercial harvesting. However, there are four Oregon bays (see chart highlighted in green) that offer five or more of the popular bay clam species: gaper, butter, cockle, littleneck, softshell and purple varnish. Most tenured clammers generally target butter, cockles and gaper clams, which make these four favored bays popular. Some also have the prized Razor Clam, at or near the bays' entrances to the ocean.

Each of these bays has its own unique attributes. Some have abundant non-native purple varnished clams, which can be great fun to dig and you can keep up to 72. Kids love digging these clams. Other bays might be in close proximity or offer larger clams or an abundance of your favorite species. Most are easy to reach by car or truck. Some of these bays are easily accessed by car and also offer boat launches where you can get to areas by boat less frequented.

When you're done clamming, most Oregon bays also offer great crabbing. You can catch crabs from a boat, the dock and even from shore. Many bays have marinas that rent boats and everything else you need for a successful crabbing venture.

There are other bays that can be just as awesome, depending on your preferences for location, species, abundance and other possible excursions for the day. Some of the less frequented areas that require boat access can offer a greater abundance of clams, too. Fortunately, in Oregon, you have a lot of choices.

Washington's Limitless Bays

With over 10,000 streams, 15 major rivers and 19 major watersheds all feeding into the Puget Sound, there are countless areas to go bay clamming. The Washington Department of Fish and Wildlife (WDFW) has over 400 areas listed for bay clams on their website at www.wdfw. wa.gov. These are grouped into seventeen marine areas, all with varying regulations and season schedules, often differing by location and species. This doesn't include the Indian Reservations, National Parks and private lands, some with their own regulations and season schedules. If you are new to Washington clamming, it's best to spend some time on their website or pick up the WDFW seasons and regulations handbook.

There are two ocean bays in Washington: North Bay and Willapa Bay. Willapa Bay is located near the

Best Oregon Bays

The locations listed in green are the largest bays and offer the most species: Geoducks, by far, are the hardest clams to find in the Oregon intertidal zones and require at least a -2.0 or lower tide. In some years, the tides don't get that low. Clamming for geoducks in Oregon takes planning, identification and digging skills. Since geoducks are easier to harvest in Washington, it's a great place to learn, prior to harvesting on the rare < -2.0 tide Oregon.

OREGON BAYS & BAY CLAM SPECIES	Necanicum	Nehalem	Tillamook	Netarts	Nestucca	Siletz	Yaquina	Alsea	Siuslaw	Umpqua	Coos	Coquille
Gaper, Blue & Horse			●	●			●				●	
Butter, Quahog Martha Washington			●	●			●				●	
Cockle, Basket			●	●			●					
Littleneck, Manila			●	●			●					
Softshell, Eastern, Mud	●	●	●	●	●	●	●	●	●	●	●	●
Purple Varnish, Mahogany	●	●	●	●	●	●	●	●				
Razor Clam	●		●	●					●		●	
Geoduck				●							●	

Best Washington Bays

A list of the most frequented areas for Bay Clamming in Washington. If you are looking to conquer the geoduck clam, I've listed two areas in green that are popular places to start and observe geoduck clammers.

WASHINGTON BAYS & BAY CLAM SPECIES	Willapa Bay	Quilcene Bay	Duckabush	Dosewallips	Shine Tidelands	Oak Bay Park	Fort Flagler State Park	Sequim Bay	South Indian Beach	Birch Bay
Geoduck			●	●	●	●	●		●	
Gaper, Blue & Horse			●	●	●	●	●		●	●
Butter, Quahog Martha Washington			●	●	●	●	●	●	●	●
Cockle, Basket	●		●	●	●	●	●	●	●	●
Littleneck, Manila	●	●	●	●	●	●	●	●	●	●
Softshell, Eastern, Mud	●	●					●			
Purple Varnish, Mahogany	●					●	●	●	●	●
Oyster	●	●	●	●	●		●	●	●	●

Oregon border only 35 miles from Seaside, Oregon. Willapa Bay is unique in one respect – there is really good ocean beach Razor Clamming on the north end of the Long Beach, Washington peninsula and it's only a 10-minute drive to the east side of the peninsula (Willapa Bay's edge), where you can harvest oysters after limiting out on Razor Clams. There you will find Oysterville, where oysters take very little effort to find and harvest, in fact, they are just lying on the sand, all you have to do is pick them up!

The Puget Sound area also has a plethora of spots on private bays. If you're lucky like my nephew, whose in-laws own a vacation beach house on Whidbey Island, all you have to do is walk a few steps from your deck to reach a clammer's paradise.

Not only is there great fishing, crabbing and clamming, since it's a private bay and there are only a few neighbors that rarely go clamming, there is an abundance of clams. On one trip, we took 120 cockles in fifteen minutes. Experiences like these create unforgettable memories.

At any given time, WDFW can have fifty-plus areas listed for closure or advisory of potential closures caused by pollution or harmful toxins. Always check to see if the area you are planning to clam has been tested for safe consumption.

Washington has an overwhelming list of choices, especially if you're going for the first time or you're trying to find your first almighty geoduck. To make things easier, I've narrowed the list down to sites with these attributes:

1. Open to the Public
2. Easy Access
3. No Boat Required
4. Well Managed by Washington Department of Fish and Wildlife
5. An Abundance of Clams
6. Most enhanced by The WDFW Clam & Oyster Enhancement Program

I've clammed at most of these areas (see page 62), the other recommendations are from friends, family and a few WDFW game wardens. WDFW has an amazing website for shellfish, possibly the best in North America. Pick an area and you can get information telling you where to go in the bay or estuary specifically for the species you're after. In some cases, they have even set markers to help you find specific spots. A few also give tide advice, and some areas will even point out where they have enhanced the geoduck population.

If you want to take your first geoduck adventure both Dosewallips State Park and Duckabush are good spots. On a low tide, you can observe experienced clammers finding and digging geoducks with success. And with a little luck, you could even leave with your first limit of three geoducks.

Don't get overwhelmed by all the choices. All of these are great places to start and the information you need is at your fingertips.

WHEN TO GO BAY CLAMMING

Just like with Razor Clamming, tides are very important to successful bay clamming. If you have not already read "When to Go Razor Clamming" on page 16, I highly recommend it because that information applies here too.

Bay Clamming is open all year in Oregon. However, Washington has limited times and dates scheduled for each species and location. It takes a little more effort to research what is open and when, some of which is covered under the "Shellfish Species and Regulations" on page 81. You will find much more detailed information on the WDFW website and in their Fishing Regulations Handbook.

Razor Clams spawn when water temperatures get to 55 degrees, which is usually around late summer. Consequently, from Tillamook Head in Seaside, Oregon through Long Beach, Washington, Razor Clamming is closed from July 15th through September 30th. For that reason, during this period of wonderful weather in the Pacific Northwest, I prefer to go Bay Clamming. If you are lucky enough to be near any of the many bays and estuaries along the Pacific Northwest Coast or Puget Sound area, you have the opportunity to go Bay Clamming (and oystering in WA) in some of the most fertile clamming beds found anywhere.

Clamming in bays is a nice break from Razor Clamming because there is so much life to discover in these beautiful bays and estuaries. Yes, some areas are muddy and you're most likely going to get your hands dirty but it's well worth the effort.

The weather is almost always good during this period. I have seen so many beautiful summer mornings and summer sunsets while bay clamming.

KEY DIFFERENCES FROM RAZOR CLAMMING

What Time to Show Up: With Razor Clams, I always recommend going two hours early and following the surf out to low tide. Although you can do this with Bay Clamming, I've observed better Bay Clam shows from low tide to high tide. When Bay Clamming, I usually go thirty minutes before or just at low tide depending on the species I'm after.

Tide Depths: Take a look at the species depth chart listed on the next page. Many people like steamer clams – littlenecks, manila, softshell and possibly purple varnish clams. Many of these species live at higher tide levels within the intertidal zone (area between high tide and low tide), this means you can leave later or clam longer as the tide rises. If you don't need a minus tide there will be more days when you can clam; this is very different from Razor Clamming.

Different Bays: Different bays offer different species. More importantly, how high up in the intertidal zone clams can be found and at what time the tide is the lowest can vary greatly. Always make sure you have tide information specific to the bay you are clamming. The low tide in Coos Bay can be much later than the low tide in Willapa Bay, for example.

After a little experience, you will discover you don't need a very low tide in many bays. A few good examples are Netarts Bay in Oregon, or the Shine Tidelands in the Puget Sound area where you can find littleneck clams in areas with a three-foot tide (that is a + 3.0 tide). So, depending on the bay and species you're after, you may not need a very low tide. If you're a beginner, pick the lowest tides and after a while you'll figure out when you can get your limit in upper intertidal zones at even plus tides, not just minus tides.

Geoducks: If you're going after geoducks in Oregon, I only know of two bays – Netarts and Coos Bay – that have them in the intertidal zone, and it's not worth trying unless you have a -2.0 tide or greater. That is a very low tide for these areas, occurring maybe a day or two a year, some years none at all. Washington is lucky enough to have at least ten areas with geoducks, but you still need a -2.0 tide or better. Geoducks can be found in most all of the larger, northwestern bays in the subtidal zone (always under water) in depths up to 60 fathoms or more. If you're not going to be scuba diving, you're only option to bag the elusive geoduck is a very low tide.

Species, Tides and Depths

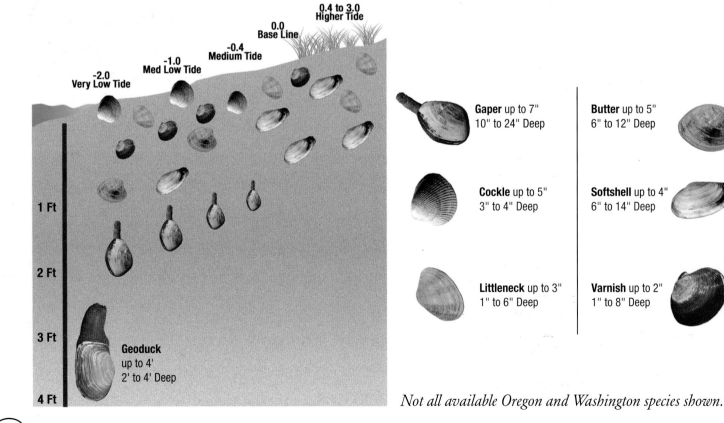

Not all available Oregon and Washington species shown.

Bay Clam Details & Shows

Once Bay Clam larvae find a home in the sand they move very little in their lifetime. Even if they have a large enough foot to bury down in the sand most won't move; if they do move it's horizontally and it takes them a very long time. For the most part, they are just stuck in the mud. They will move their necks, especially the clams with large necks. Once they find a large show, experienced clammers stick their finger in the show hole to make the neck retract, then they insert a stick to ensure the clam retracts its neck all the way. The stick provides the clam's location and a marker for digging around, making it easier to harvest the clam with its shell intact.

Often you'll be faced with many holes, especially if there are ghost shrimp holes which are similar to a Gaper Clam hole, making things a little confusing for first-time clammers. There can be debris or pellets (called pseudo feces) around a legitimate show, which happens when the clam's filtration system pumps out water. This debris is a good indication there is a clam below.

Finding Bay Clam shows is much easier than finding Razor Clam shows so most people don't bother to pound the surf's edge. However, if I'm trying to find large clams, sometimes I'll get out as far as I can and do a little pounding on the sand. Once they're disturbed, large Bay Clams will move their necks, creating a show (some will spit at you as well) just like Razor Clams.

Usually you'll see other clammers when you get to a bay, which is a good sign that you will find clams.

TYPICAL SHOW

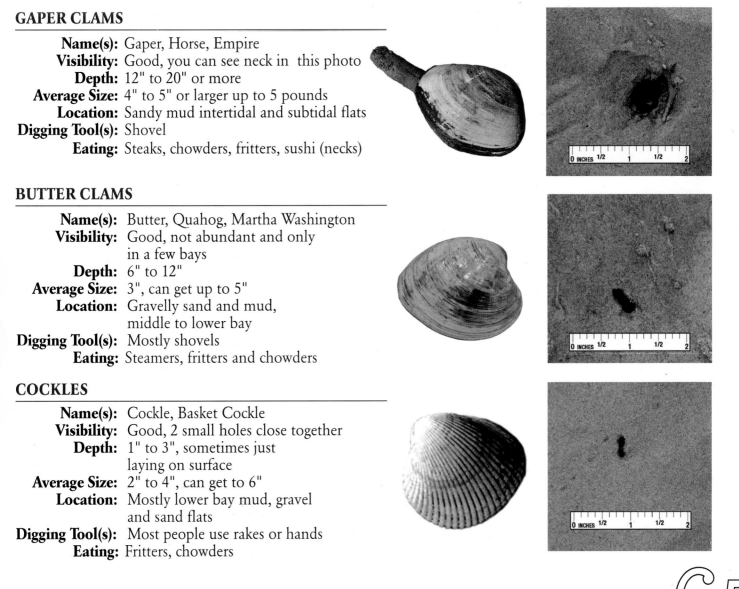

GAPER CLAMS

Name(s):	Gaper, Horse, Empire
Visibility:	Good, you can see neck in this photo
Depth:	12" to 20" or more
Average Size:	4" to 5" or larger up to 5 pounds
Location:	Sandy mud intertidal and subtidal flats
Digging Tool(s):	Shovel
Eating:	Steaks, chowders, fritters, sushi (necks)

BUTTER CLAMS

Name(s):	Butter, Quahog, Martha Washington
Visibility:	Good, not abundant and only in a few bays
Depth:	6" to 12"
Average Size:	3", can get up to 5"
Location:	Gravelly sand and mud, middle to lower bay
Digging Tool(s):	Mostly shovels
Eating:	Steamers, fritters and chowders

COCKLES

Name(s):	Cockle, Basket Cockle
Visibility:	Good, 2 small holes close together
Depth:	1" to 3", sometimes just laying on surface
Average Size:	2" to 4", can get to 6"
Location:	Mostly lower bay mud, gravel and sand flats
Digging Tool(s):	Most people use rakes or hands
Eating:	Fritters, chowders

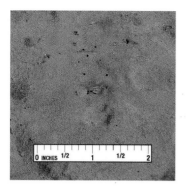

LITTLENECK AND MANILA CLAMS

Name(s):	Littleneck, Manila (very similar clams)
Visibility:	Very small holes, can be hard to see
Depth:	1" to 4", many times in colonies
Average Size:	2" to 3"
Location:	Can be very high through low intertidal zones
Digging Tool(s):	Rake, shovel, hands (even in high tides)
Eating:	Most popular steamer clams

PURPLE VARNISH CLAMS

Name(s):	Purple Varnish, Mahogany
Visibility:	Multiple small holes
Depth:	1" to 8", most in colonies
Average Size:	1" to 3", mostly 2" or less
Location:	Sand, mud, gravel, medium to high bay areas
Digging Tool(s):	Shovel and hands (hard to see in mud)
Eating:	Steamers (but hard to purge), fritters

SOFTSHELL CLAMS

Name(s):	Softshell, Longnecks, Eastern Mud Clam
Visibility:	Most abundant clam, some in colonies
Depth:	6" to 12"
Average Size:	2" to 4", can get up to 5"
Location:	Mud flats, gravelly mud, upper to middle bay
Digging Tool(s):	Shovel, if in mud or sand a gun will work
Eating:	Fritters, small ones make good steamers

GEODUCK

Name(s):	Geoduck, King Clam (may be largest in world)
Visibility:	Very similar to Gaper show, can be larger
Depth:	Most at 3' to 4', can be deeper
Average Size:	1 to 3 pounds average, up to 7 pounds
Location:	Select bays at tides lower than -2.0 feet
Digging Tool(s):	Large trash can and shovel (challenging)
Eating:	Siphon raw (e.g. sushi), mantle cooked

How to Dig Bay Clams

Digging Bay Clams is easier than Razor Clamming. Don't get me wrong, you're going to get muddy and it can be a workout depending on which species you're digging, but Bay Clams don't dig downward. For lack of a better term they are "stuck in the mud". Once you've identified a show, you can take your time, your clam is in there somewhere. Many Bay Clams colonize, so once you find one clam keep enlarging the hole until you find more of them.

Bay clamming is a pretty laid-back affair. Many clammers just wear their gardening attire, and bring a garden shovel, rake and pale. The best thing about Bay Clamming is that you can take the entire family and use what most of us have available in the garage. If you already have a Razor Clam shovel, I recommend using it for a number of Bay Clams, like the Gaper Clam. If you find softshell and other clams in a sandy tidal flat,

a Razor Clam gun will work, too. The biggest challenge is not breaking the shells so, in most cases, you want to dig to the side of the clam show. Clams like cockles have a very short neck and need to be very close to the surface to feed, so when you are in sand or mud, you might only need your hands to dig. Sometimes you will see their shells sticking out of the surface.

After you learn to dig one species it's not hard to figure out how to dig for them all (with the possible exception of geoducks). The following pages describe in detail how to dig a Gaper Clam; the rest of the instructions are abbreviated, because the differences between clams are minimal. For example, Gapers are pretty deep so you use the same method for Butter Clams, except they are usually closer to the surface. Cockles and Purple Varnish Clams colonize, so you will often see multiple clam shows grouped together.

Digging Gaper Clams

Sometimes you will be overwhelmed by the number of shows you see in the sand. If you want to know whether it's a true show remember that when clams feed there can be debris or pellets (pseudo feces) adjacent to the show, caused by water pumping out through the siphon. With larger clams, you can stick your finger in the hole and touch the neck and feel it retract.

To avoid damaging your clam, place a stick in the clam show to retract the neck and leave it as a marker. Stick or no stick, dig to the side of the show. If you're a beginner, use your hands so as not to break the shell. As you get more experienced, you'll learn the safe zone when digging around the clam.

3

Keep in mind that the smaller the clam neck, the closer it has to be to the surface to feed. In general, clams with a short neck (like cockles) are closer to the surface, and larger clams with long necks are deeper in the sand or mud. Small clams close to the surface are easy to miss, sift through the sand you've dug before giving up on your prize.

4

This Gaper, with its large neck, is over 18" deep. This is my nephew Grant, who knows how to be careful with the shovel. He can feel even the slightest rub on the clam's shell and once he can see the clam, he uses his hands to dislodge it.

5

Gaper's can be up to 2' deep, as you dig deeper enlarge the circumference of the hole. For wet sand, a bucket with no bottom positioned over the hole will prevent the sides from falling in.

Geoducks requiring a -2.0 or better tide, can be 4' deep, sometimes requiring a garbage can with the bottom cut out to prevent sides from falling in.

6

Grant finally gets his prize, a bigger than average Gaper Clam for sure! You can keep 12 in Oregon and 7 in Washington, that's a lot of clam meat.

Remember, you're not done until you fill your hole back in. You have to reach the shore with the entire clam, you cannot clean them on the beach and leave the shell behind.

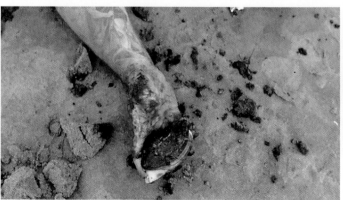

Digging Purple Varnish Clams

Purple Varnish Clams are not a native species and started populating two Pacific Northwest bays about twenty years ago. The number of areas where they can be found continues to spread and you can now find them in most Oregon and Washington bays. In more recent years they have also started populating the Puget Sound area and I have found them in abundance all over Whidbey Island.

In Oregon there is a very popular spot in Lincoln City, Siletz Bay on the south edge of the city. Go to the roadside on the north end of the Bay House Restaurant and look for people clamming out on the bay. Although Siletz Bay also has Softshell Clams, first-time clammers love digging Purple Varnish Clams here because you don't need too low a tide and you can take up to 72 clams per person.

Clamming for Purple Varnish Clams provides fun for the whole family, and all you need is a garden shovel, a pale and a license. They have a fairly small show (1/16" to 1/8"), but when you find one, you usually find many more in the same spot. These clams generally live in colonies between 1" to 8" below the surface. It will be muddy so you're going to get dirty, but you can wear tennis shoes, rubber boots or waders if you have them.

Just remember, when digging go slow to prevent breakage and because these clams are small make sure you don't miss any in the sand or mud you dig up. I see people leaving clams behind all the time.

Digging Softshell Clams

Available in all coastal Oregon and Washington bays, Softshell Clams are one of the most abundant clams in the Pacific Northwest. The Softshell Clam has a hole very similar to a Gaper Clam, so they are easily confused. They are smaller than Gaper Clams and have a shorter neck, so they are found closer to the surface.

They're called Softshell because their shells are thinner and more brittle than Gaper Clams, but their shells are not as thin as Razor Clams. They love gravelly mud and like upper bay areas so they don't need a very low tide.

Use the same digging method as you would a Gaper Clam, but remember they are easier to break and are found closer to the surface. The smaller clams can be prepared as steamer clams, just make sure you remove the sock (membrane around the neck) after steaming them and before you dunk them in butter. I use the larger ones in fritters.

Digging Cockle Clams

Cockles live closer to the surface than any other clam. Each hole in their siphon leaves a show so a single Cockle can have two side by side, pea-sized or smaller holes.

In some rocky areas you'll need a rake. Cockles also like sandy mud and eel grass, where you can occasionally see them on the surface. When they are on the surface, sticking part way out of the surface, or an inch below the surface, you can use your hands.

Digging Butter Clams

Butter Clams leave a very particular show that looks like someone stuck a flat-head screw driver into the ground. They are typically less than a foot deep and most people use a shovel or rake, depending on whether they are in mud or gravel.

Butter Clams are more plentiful in Washington, but they are found in a few Oregon bays. Finding and digging for them is very similar to Gaper Clams.

Digging Littleneck and Manila Clams

Littleneck and Manila Clams share a lot of similarities. However, Manila Clams are more often found in the Puget Sound area, even in unusually high areas in the intertidal zone. Both make fantastic steamer clams and are what is usually served in local restaurants. They look similar to Cockles, but they are smaller and found deeper (5" to 10") below the surface. Littleneck and Manila Clams enjoy some of the same habitat so you might run into a few of them together, but Littlenecks prefer the coarse, muddier areas of the bay. Sometimes you'll need a rake with these clams, but I generally use a shovel. These seem to be more scarce in some Oregon bays and better in Washington bays that also offer a few more species of these small popular clams.

Digging Geoduck Clams

The Geoduck is arguably the largest clam in the world and they can live up to 150 years old! The WDFW website states that the oldest Geoduck on record lived a whopping 168 years. They are expensive to buy in the U.S. because on the Asian market they go for up to $300 per clam. In China it's considered an aphrodisiac and is served as sashimi or sushi.

In order to harvest a Geoduck, you need a tide of -2.0 or better in both Oregon and Washington. Although they are farmed and harvested on public beaches in Washington, they are only occasionally found in Oregon (i.e., Netarts Bay and Coos Bays). Finding these clams is difficult and harvesting them is time-consuming. Some people mark the show by placing a lengthy dowel in the hole. Geoducks have a very long siphon, it can be over 3 feet long, and they are 3' to 4' below the surface. The most difficult part is keeping the walls of your digging hole from collapsing. Many clammers use a bottomless 30-gallon bucket or garbage can and dig the mud/sand out from the center of it while continuing to push the can in deeper. However, for many, a can this size is not large enough. Sporting goods stores in Washington sell 4-foot metal cylinders, and it is not uncommon to see clammers using galvanized garbage cans with the bottom cut out.

There is also the issue of water filling the hole. These clams are at the deepest part of the intertidal zone, where the sand can contain a lot of water. Many people use an old coffee can or a shrimp gun to remove the water. I like using a shrimp gun because you can keep pumping out water even if the hole's filling up quickly.

The trick to digging Geoducks is removing as much sand, silt and mud from your hole as you can – while the sides are falling in and your hole continuously fills up with water. This clam takes some planning and determination, but when you do get one it's like bagging a seven-point elk or 60-pound salmon.

Cleaning Bay Clams

You just spent the day Bay Clamming and now you have a bucketful of the little treasures. So what do you do with them? The clams that you don't want to steam, barbeque, or eat raw from the shell can be cleaned in the same way as a Razor Clam. Since Bay Clam species have similar anatomy, when you know how to clean one, it's easy to figure out how to clean the rest. I will walk you through the steps for cleaning a Gaper Clam, because it's similar enough to how you clean all bay clams.

If you've ever had steamers in the shell, cooked live in beer or wine with a little butter, you know they are fantastic! But finding sand or grit in your steamers will quickly ruin your meal. Clams suck in water and push out waste and sand, this is called purging. Almost all clams purchased from the market have been purged. So when you're harvesting them on your own, you'll have to purge them yourself.

I've mentioned eating raw clams, which isn't done much in the Pacific Northwest but it's common on the East Coast. In Oregon, I rarely see people eat raw Butter Clams, but on the East Coast I've eaten them this way frequently. You brave souls here in the Pacific Northwest might want to give it a try. Just remember, you must keep your clams alive through the purging process and until you eat them. Don't ever eat a dead clam, especially a raw dead clam, and make sure that the area where you harvested them was tested and approved by the department of fish and wildlife and state health department.

PURGING BAY CLAMS

On the internet you will find plenty of information on how to purge Bay Clams. Unfortunately, there is a lot of misinformation and with so many different opinions it can be very confusing. However, purging clams is super easy if you follow some basic rules. Human beings have been doing it for hundreds, if not thousands, of years and you can do it too. After all, the only goal is not to kill the clam, and clams are pretty tough!

So stop the purging madness! I'm going to list the controversial techniques you'll hear from family, friends, cookbooks, chefs and on the internet. Then share what I believe are best practices for purging your clams.

- **CORNMEAL:** There is a long-standing debate about adding cornmeal to the water you are soaking your clams in. The idea is that clams eat the cornmeal and purge out whatever else is in their stomach. This process has been passed down by generations and if you want to purge your clams this way there is nothing wrong with it. However, clams are happier sucking in sea water and if they really do suck cornmeal in, you will be eating the cornmeal from their stomachs. Who wants that? In my experience, cornmeal doesn't improve the purge process and most of it falls to the bottom of the bucket anyway. I have seen no evidence that clams purge better with additives like cornmeal. My grandma did this, and many swear by it, but I do not.

Best Practice: Don't use any additives when purging your clams. How long you purge, changing the water and having the correct amount of sea salt are the critical factors for hard to purge clams.

- **SALT:** The internet, cookbooks, even some chefs will tell you to add regular table salt to your purging water. I've noticed that this has actually shortened the life of my clams and, at minimum, it extends the amount of time it takes to purge the clams. Think about it, you take your clams out of sea water, which has just the right ratio of salt to water. Then, drop them in water with iodized salt and a different salt to water ratio, what a shocker for the clam. And that's not taking into consideration the fact that most people use chlorinated water.

Best Practice: When done harvesting, fill your bucket with sea water from where the clams were harvested. This way you will know that the water has the proper conditions for keeping these clams happy, including the perfect temperature. If you don't take sea water, when you get home use only dechlorinated water. Add enough sea salt to make the water as salty as the ocean, this is very important, 1/2 cup sea salt or more per gallon. If you purge for an extended period you'll need to empty the bucket to get rid of all the debris and increase the oxygen, then refill it again. If your water is as "salty as the sea" and you change your water often enough the clams will purge completely.

• **TIME:** I've read that all clams only need an hour or two to purge, but clams eat and filter at different rates. As a general rule, I'll purge my clams at least overnight. My experience has been that clams coming from light sand need less time. Clams coming from a heavy mud substrate can take much longer. For example, I need three days to purge Purple Varnish Clams harvested in the muddy substrate of Siletz Bay and I change the water three times (also oxygenate the water).

Best Practice: If you are purging a particular species for the first time, change the water when you think they are done purging and then check on them four to six hours later. If there is any additional debris at the bottom of the bucket, they're not done purging. Next time, you'll know how much time it takes to purge that particular species, from the specific environment you harvested them.

• **TEMPERATURE:** Many people put their clams on ice or add ice to the water. Temperature is very important! Your clams were comfortable at the temperature they were in when you harvested them. If the water was 60°F and you put them in water that is 35°F you will slow the rate at which they purge or, worse, the shock could kill them. If you throw your clams into the cooler with ice on the bottom and then pour ice over them, they can freeze to death.

Best Practice: If you take sea water from where you harvested them, the water temperature will be perfect. If you don't, be mindful about where you harvested them and the temperature of the water. Was it a warm summer day or a very cold winter day? Keep the water temperature as close as you can to where the clams came from. Cool down the water by putting them in a refrigerator or adding ice to the sides of your bucket (don't just throw a bunch of ice into the water).

• **SUBMERGING YOUR CLAMS FOR EXTENDED PERIODS:** I often hear people giving advice on purging clams for extended periods, with no mention of oxygen. Clam processing plants purge clams for days but they also oxygenate the water. If you need to purge for an extended period of time, the clams need oxygen, especially if your clam to water ratio is high (lots of clams in a little water use up the oxygen

quicker than a few clams in a lot of water). If your clams start opening up, they might be suffocating.

Best Practice: For extended purge periods, even overnight, at the minimum you need to shake and stir the water to aerate it. Better yet, replace the water a couple of times or buy a fish tank air pump (mine cost $8.00). With the air pump, I don't have to worry about the clams and I can purge for days if I choose.

• **LIDS AND ICE:** Many people just toss their harvested clams in a cooler with ice and shut the lid. This is a bad idea for several reasons, first the lid will suffocate them, then the ice will freeze them and when it melts, it will drown the clams at the bottom.

Best Practice: If using a dry cooler, remember that clams need oxygen, moisture, an appropriate temperature, and to prevent them from drowning place a cloth at the bottom of the cooler. As previously mentioned, it is best to take them home in the sea water where you harvested them, that way you also get a head start on purging them on your way home. Bring extra sea water home for changing the water during purging.

• **OPEN SHELLS ARE IMPORTANT:** Bay Clams close their shell when they sense danger. If the clam doesn't try to stay closed when you pinch the shell or shut it with your fingers, it's probably no longer alive. Always throw out dead clams.

Best Practice: Most clams will stick their necks out while purging so it's easy to know if they are alive. If in question, give them a squeeze, touch their necks, test them for any signs of life, before just tossing them out.

You have to keep your clams alive. Clams are pretty tough. That's why there are so many approaches that people use when transporting and purging their clams. However, people don't generally think about "best practices" which impact the time it takes to purge their clams or ensure their clams have purged completely. By using "best practices" you can extend the life of the clam to 3 days or more. You'll never have to eat another sandy clam again.

A comfortable clam will stay alive longer, purge faster and purge more completely. The variables are water, temperature and oxygen. The closer to the environment where you harvested them, the more efficiently they will take in water and push out the debris in their stomachs.

Clean or Purge?

You must purge clams of all sand and debris when eating them raw, steamed or barbequed in the shell. Some people don't like to eat any clam that is larger than a few inches without cutting it open and cleaning it out. It's your choice on how you eat your clams.

If you are new to all of this, it can be kind of confusing. You can open and clean any clam, this is what I do most often. Purging is for when you want to eat your clams whole. All clams will purge themselves of debris, but some better than others. For example, when found in heavy mud the Purple Varnish Clam is more difficult to purge. So sometimes we purge them, other times we'll clean them.

Keep in mind these are my preferred methods and depending on how you want to eat them they can be done either way.

BAY CLAM SPECIES	Pump Clean by Purging	Cut Open Clean Out Meat	Drop in Boiling Water to Deshell	Purged Clams in Shells Can be Frozen for Future Steamers
Geoduck		●	●	
Razor Clam		●	●	
Gaper, Blue & Horse		●	●	
Butter, Quahog Martha Washington	●	●		
Cockle, Basket	●	●		
Littleneck, Manila	●			●
Softshell, Eastern, Mud	●	●	●	●
Purple Varnish, Mahogany	●	●	●	●

CLEANING BAY CLAMS

Gapers, Cockles, Butter, Softshell, Littlenecks and numerous other bay clams all have similar anatomy. Cleaning is basically the same for each species. The only differences are that some clams have more meat than others (larger or smaller neck, mantel or foot) and how you decide to deshell your clams. Many people shuck them with a knife. I like to boil the clams for 15 seconds or freeze them for ten minutes until their shells open. Other than that, what follows can be applied to most any Bay Clam.

How to Clean a Gaper Clam

1. Soak in Sea Water: Soak Gapers in their own sea water (or 3/4 cup sea salt for each gallon of distilled water) for a few hours and their necks will extend for easier cleaning.

2. Boil to Deshell: You can use a knife to cut down the inside of each shell or boil the clam just until the shell pops open (about 10 to 20 seconds). If you use a netted clam bag, you can do many clams in one dunk.

3. Quickly Cool Meat: It is important not to cook the clam in the boiling water. Dunk for as short a period as possible. Right after removal, place the clams in cold water.

4. Remove Shell: Even after boiling, a Gaper Clam might not just slide out of the shell. If it doesn't, insert a knife and cut the membrane that's still stuck to the shell.

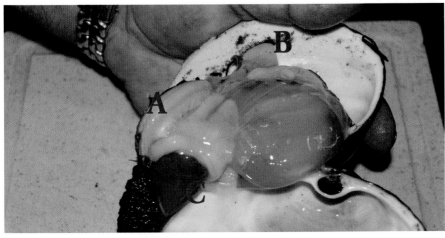

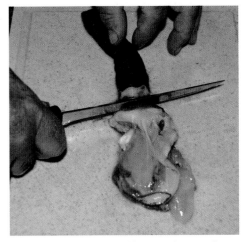

5. Clam Anatomy, Edible Meat: Once the clam is open, look at its anatomy. There are basically three sections that provide the meat:

A. The mantel or belly, **B.** The digger or foot, **C.** The neck. The neck can be used for many things. The foot and belly are generally chopped or minced.

6. Cut the Neck Off: Cut the neck where the mantel and body start. Finding a small pea crab in the shell is normal, just discard it.

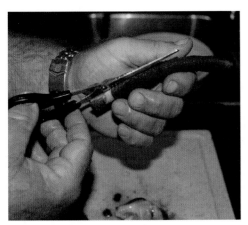

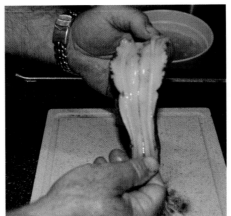

7. Cut Up Siphon Holes: Snip 1/4 to 1/2 inch off the clam siphon tip. There are two syphon holes, cut each hole from the bottom up to open the neck up all the way and fillet it.

8. Butterfly Neck: Once the neck is open, find a corner and strip off the neck membrane. If you want, use your knife to scrape the neck membrane.

9. Clean Neck: If the neck skin is difficult to pull off or it is discolored, use sea salt to scrub it. You can scrub with sea salt until the neck is white, but it's not required.

11. Clean Gaper Meat: It is pretty easy to distinguish the meat from what is to be discarded in each species. It will be very similar to what you see here. The neck (top), foot on the left, mantel or belly on the right.

10. Cut and Wash: Carefully cut the belly and mantel away from the stomach, then the foot, leaving two pieces. Wash the entire clam well and discard the remains.

Refrigerating and Freezing Your Clams

REFRIGERATING PURGED CLAMS

Once your clams are purged, you want to keep them alive until it's time to eat them. Clams need to breathe in your refrigerator so put them in a wire mesh strainer, a colander, something that allows oxygen in. Refrigerator fans can dry clams out so placing a wet towel on top and a dry towel underneath to soak up any dripping water. Pretty simple, just like when you buy clams at the grocery store and bring them home to refrigerate.

Nothing is better than cooking your clams the same day you harvest them but that is not always possible. If cared for properly, purged clams can stay alive in the refrigerator for a day and much longer depending on the species. The more tightly the clam can shut its shell the longer it will live. For example, the Purple Varnish Clam is known for how tightly it can close its shell and I've kept them alive in my refrigerator for two weeks, Butter Clams a week, Littlenecks and Manilas for five days. Softshell Clams can't close their shells all the way and have exposed meat that will dry out, so eat them as soon as they're done purging.

This is somewhat academic since clams freeze very well. If you are not going to eat your clams right away, freeze them! Most clams (like steamers) freeze really well in the shell for later use. When you take them out to cook them, they will open up their shells just like fresh steamer clams.

REFRIGERATING CLEANED CLAM MEAT

If your clams aren't steamers or you're not going to eat them raw, you don't need to purge them. You do need to cut open and clean them like a Razor or Gaper Clam. I always try to clean these clams the same day I harvest them. However, as long as you keep them alive, you don't have to clean them the same day. When you do clean them always throw out any dead clams.

Once cleaned, store the clam meat in a closed container (i.e., freezer bag or plastic container) and refrigerate. Cleaned clam meat is good in your fridge for a few days but it's best to eat it as soon as possible.

FREEZING CLAM MEAT

To freeze cleaned clam meat, add the clam liquor (juices) to the freezer bags when you can to deter freezer burn. I prefer not to use water, I believe it dilutes the flavor. Squeeze the air out of the bag and you can freeze them with optimal quality for three months. If you use a vacuum sealer, you can get a good seal by freezing the open vacuum bag for fifteen minutes before vacuum sealing.

If you vacuum seal and deep freeze your clam meat (at 0° or below) it will last even longer. I've done this and had clams last for up to 6 months, and occasionally I've gone even longer with pretty good results.

RAW, STUFF, STEAM, CHOWDER OR FRY? My family doesn't like to waste a beautiful Razor Clam by putting it into a chowder. Or, use a Cockle for steamer clams, way too tough and salty. That said, many clammers and great chefs don't always agree with us. James Beard, a famous chef from Gearhart, Oregon, is a good example. When he lived in Gearhart he made his chowder from Razor Clams. You can find the recipe in his cookbook and it's a fantastic clam chowder. We just prefer to fry our Razor Clams because there is no better clam to fry in the world.

Everyone has their favorite way to cook clams. The chart below is how we like to use our clams. If you're new to clamming this chart can be helpful in deciding how to cook whatever species you have harvested.

BEST USE When Cooking Bay Clams	FRIED CLAM STEAK	STUFFED OR CASINO	SASHIMI, SUSHI, CEVICHE	RAW ON HALF SHELL	STEAMER	BARBEQUE	PASTA SAUCES, CHOWDERS, FRITTERS
Geoduck			Neck ●				Body ●
Razor Clam	●						
Gaper, Blue & Horse	Neck ●		Neck ●				●
Butter, Quahog, Martha Washington		●		●		●	●
Cockle Basket		●					●
Littleneck, Manila				●	●	●	
Softshell, Eastern, Mud		● Large			●	●	●
Purple Varnish, Mahogany					●		●

Bay Clam
Recipes

Bay Clam Fritters

INGREDIENTS

2 cups chopped clams
   (your choice)
2 cups flour
3/4 cup milk
3/4 cup clam liquor (or beer)
2 eggs
4-6 green onions, chopped
2 stalks celery, chopped small
1/2 cup diced sweet onion
1 teaspoon baking powder
Salt to taste
1/2 inch canola oil
Sliced lemon
Malt vinegar
Tartar sauce

1. Clam species of your choice, or a combination of species, cleaned and chopped. Reserve the liquor to use later in the recipe.
2. Chop green onions and celery, dice onion, set aside.
3. Mix flour and baking powder. Beat eggs, milk and clam juice, then stir into flour mixture. Add chopped clams and other ingredients. If necessary, add more milk to create a batter of the right consistency. Use a tablespoon to create fritter size of your choice.
4. Salt mixture to taste.
5. Add about 1/2 inch of oil to pan, heat close to smoke point about 350° to 375 degrees. To keep oil hot, don't add too many fritters to the pan at one time.
6. Cook until golden brown, about 2 minutes on each side. Make sure batter is cooked, but clams are not overcooked and tough. If your fritters are not getting brown fast enough (making clams tough), add a little butter to the oil.
7. Add lemon wedges and/or tartar sauce. Enjoy!

Grandma's Favorite Clam Chowder

INGREDIENTS

4 cups chopped clams of your choice
1/2 cup bacon cut into 1/2-inch pieces
2 cups celery, diced
1 cup onions, diced
1 1/2 cups carrots, diced
4 cups potatoes, diced
Salt and pepper (to taste)
4 cups clam stock (or substitute with clam base)

4 tablespoons butter
3-4 tablespoons flour
2 cups milk
2 cups half and half
1 teaspoon chicken bouillon
Parsley for garnish

1. In a large pot cook bacon pieces until brown, do not drain fat. Remove some bacon pieces for later garnish.
2. Sauté onions, carrots and celery in bacon fat until translucent.
3. Add 1/2 the butter and melt to make a roux. Slowly stir in flour, stirring occasionally. Cook until roux is mixed well and starts to thicken. For a thicker chowder use a little more flour.
4. Pour in the clam stock. Clam stock can be liquid from canned clams, freezer bags, or clam juice purchased in stores. If you prefer to use a clam base (available in some stores) you can make one by pureeing 1 cup clam meat, 1/4 cup clam juice, 2 tablespoons lemon juice and 1 teaspoon salt. Add water or clam juice to make 4 cups total.

5. Add potatoes and chicken bouillon, simmer until potatoes are tender.
6. Add clams, milk, half and half, salt and pepper to taste (for a richer, creamier chowder use 4 cups of half and half, no milk).
7. Serve hot with bread or oyster crackers with crumbled bacon on top of each serving.

More On Tides

"Time and Tide Wait for No Man"
Our motto at www.razorclamming.com

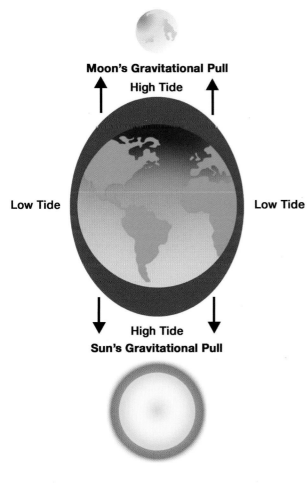

Moon's Gravitational Pull

High Tide

Low Tide   **Low Tide**

High Tide

Sun's Gravitational Pull

See "When to Go Razor Clamming" on page 16 to learn how to read a tide book and better understand intertidal and subtidal tide zones.

How Reliable Are Tide Predictions?

Tide books are pretty accurate. Tides are based on the collection of location-specific tide data from the past, celestial predictions and weather. Obviously historical is highly accurate. Astronomical forces, as seen here in this chart, are differences in the gravitational pull of the sun and moon and the speed of the earth's rotation, that ultimately create four separate tides in any given 24-hour period. For the most part, these are reoccurring events with slight deviations, making celestial predictions very accurate, as well. Combining this information is just mathematics (or computers crunching numbers) and it's why the tide books are pretty darn accurate, even with predictions for a year in advance.

However, significant changes in weather patterns, ocean currents, wind and barometric pressure can all change the tides a little bit, or quite a lot. Think about a hurricane sucking up water from the ocean, heavy rains flooding the bays or high winds thrashing the seas. Weather, especially stormy weather, can change conditions quickly. This is why some (not all) National Oceanic and Atmospheric Administration (NOAA) tide-monitoring stations collect this other information as well, not just past tidal and celestial data. All of this additional data is collected, correlated and crunched by computers to provide up-to-date tide predictions. This information is much more accurate and it's available to the public, for free, on the internet at tidesandcurrents.noaa.gov.

Tides Differ by Location

NOAA is always installing new solar-powered tide-monitoring stations to monitor tide data all over Oregon and Washington.

The Columbia River tides – from its mouth at the Pacific Ocean, inland to just past Portland, Oregon – are monitored by as many as 20 different NOAA tide-monitoring stations. There are roughly 30 monitoring stations within a 10-mile radius of the Columbia River's mouth. There can be a difference in tides in areas that are just a few miles apart. Read the wrong information and you could show up for clamming at the wrong time. For example, the 12th Avenue Bridge monitoring station in Seaside, Oregon can differ significantly from Seaside's beach tides.

For years, I have used the NOAA monitoring station at the North Jetty at the mouth of the Columbia River to get Seaside, Oregon Razor Clamming tides, even though it's on the Washington side of the Columbia. The North Jetty station has location factors that make it the most accurate for the Seaside, Oregon and Long Beach, Washington tides. The information is good for both locations but depending on weather conditions and other factors it can be fifteen minutes off, and sometimes more than 30 minutes, from one beach to the other. However, this is about as good as you can get and mirrors most tide books you can buy in Seaside or Long Beach. This is also why I say to be two hours early for Razor Clamming. The actual low tide might vary and on the rare day that it's 40 minutes off, you'll still have plenty of time to follow the tide out.

If you don't trust the tide information you're getting on the internet, call a local sporting goods store or hotel, it's their business to know this information.

My Best Advice About Tides

Once you know the tide, you have to decide if it looks like a good day for clamming. This can become complicated! In fact, complicated enough that you might miss out on great clamming just because you guessed the tide wrong. I know people that get the tide for the day and then monitor surfing tidal surge information, because clams feed more during days with a low tidal surge. So many factors effect clam feeding and shows that sometimes it's just hard to predict, even when there is a low tidal surge. When I am in doubt, I just go! Yes, the perfect -2.1 tide shows great promise, but the truth is sometimes even with a -2.1 tide the clams just aren't showing.

I once took my family for an "all-boys weekend clamming trip." We were about twenty minutes from our destination when someone asked what the tide was and I told them it was a 0.0 tide, not a minus tide. Boy, did I catch some hell! They could not believe I would schedule that trip on a day with a non-minus tide, but I knew there were many other factors that were all in our favor.

The next morning, we all limited out in twenty minutes. I was not surprised because all the other factors besides tide (sometimes more subjective factors) were in place.

A few considerations regarding tides when Razor Clamming:
- **A full moon can increase the number of feeding clams (as seen in tide books).**
- **A calm surf can affect how many clams are feeding (low tidal surge).**
- **Good weather vs. heavy rain can also affect feeding and the number of shows.**
- **Early season (March through May) is better for Razor Clamming than late season.**
- **Tides in early morning are better than late afternoon.**
- **The quality of the ocean water can affect how many clams are feeding.**
- **Water temperature can effect feeding.**
- **20,000 people on the beach the night before can have a negative impact on shows.**
- **Color of the ocean (clear, brownish, reddish) can affect clam feeding.**
- **Even El Niño can affect tides.**

There are many factors to consider. It's easy to overcomplicate it but all you need to do is think like a Razor Clam! Would you be more likely to feed on a very low tide on a dark, raining day with a rough surf after being trampled on by 20,000 people the evening before (like 4th of July), or on a beautiful day, with perfect conditions, even if the tide isn't that low? Don't get me wrong, the best sign for a good clamming day is a low tide but there are many other factors to determine just how low the tide really needs to be. Sometimes it's most important to be on time, follow the tide out and take your time, be patient. And sometimes, even in the last twenty minutes after the tide changes direction, on a non-minus tide, you can find shows.

CLAMMING *The Pacific Northwest Coast*

Shellfish Species and Regulations

Oregon's rules can change throughout the year. Washington's rules are more complex, cover 34 different beaches and 17 marine areas and also can change during the year. All regulations in the handbook are an interpretation of state, local and federal regulations.

Harvest Method and Restrictions
- A License is "Required" to Take Marine Shellfish for Everyone 14 and Older
- Diggers can share equipment like shovels, cylindrical tube or gun (minimum 4" wide).
- Each digger must have their own bag, bucket or container.
- Each digger must dig their own clams.
- Each digger cannot possess more than one limit of clams while in the harvest area.

All Razor, Gaper, Geoduck, Piddocks and Softshell Clams must be retained regardless of size or condition. Other unbroken clams returned only in immediate bay harvest area.

- Unlawful to remove clams from the shell before leaving the harvest area.

Licences
Shellfish licenses are required in all West Coast states. They can be purchased at sporting goods stores, bait and tackle shops and marinas anywhere in the state. If you are at the coast you will find shellfish licenses at major big-box stores (Walmart, Rite Aid, Walgreens, etc.), even some grocery stores and gas stations. Wherever you can buy a shellfish license, you will also find clam shovels, clam guns, bags and rakes.

Testing for Toxins and Harmful Algae
Clams, other shellfish, and even whales feed by filtering phytoplankton (commonly referred to as plankton) out of the ocean waters. Plankton sometimes carry microscopic algae and biological toxins that can be harmful to humans. Unfortunately, these toxins can't be destroyed by freezing or cooking. They can make you sick and, in rare cases, even be lethal.

Both Oregon and Washington routinely test for these harmful toxins and will close harvesting for a period of time until it is safe again. Closures can be for microscopic algae (often referred to as a Red Tide), biological toxins or pollution. Red Tide closures are infrequent, but they do happen. Recent closures for the entire year of Razor Clamming were in 1992, 1999, 2003, and 2015. Usually closures are for short periods of time.

Always check to make sure that Oregon and Washington Departments of Health and Agriculture, in cooperation with Oregon and Washington Departments of Fish and Wildlife, have tested for shellfish toxins and that the area you are clamming is open and safe for consumption. To find out more information on a specific area, following are contact numbers for Oregon and Washington.

SHELLFISH HOTLINE AND REGULATORY AGENCIES
- **Oregon Shellfish Safety Hotline**
  800-448-2474

- **Washington Shellfish Safety Hotline**
  800-562-5632

- **OREGON DEPARTMENT OF FISH AND WILDLIFE**
  4034 Fairview Industrial Drive SE
  Salem, OR 97302
  503-947-6000
  www.dfw.state.or.us

- **WASHINGTON DEPARTMENT OF FISH & WILDLIFE**
  1111 Washington St. SE
  Olympia, WA 98501
  360-902-2200
  www.wdfw.wa.gov

SHELLFISH SPECIES & REGULATIONS	Oregon Season	Oregon Daily Limit	Washington Season	Washington Daily Limit
Razor Clam	All Year, Except Clatsop County Beaches North of Tillamook Head Closed July 15 - Sept 30	First 15 No Matter What Size	Locations, Times and Dates Determined Month to Month. Check at www.wdfw.wa.gov	First 15 No Matter What Size
Geoduck	All Year	12	Locations, Times and Dates Determined Month to Month. Check at www.wdfw.wa.gov	3 Total, Any Size
Gaper, Blue & Horse	All Year	12	Locations, Times and Dates Determined Month to Month. Check at www.wdfw.wa.gov	7, Includes Broken
Softshell, Eastern, Mud	All Year	First 36	Locations, Times and Dates Determined Month to Month. Check at www.wdfw.wa.gov	7, Includes Broken
Butter, Quahog Martha Washington	All Year	20 Clams, 12 in Aggregate Gaper or Geoducks	Locations, Times and Dates Determined Month to Month. Check at www.wdfw.wa.gov	Min Size 1 1/2", 40, 10 lbs. Combined Total
Cockle, Basket	All Year	20 Clams, 12 in Aggregate Gaper or Geoducks	Locations, Times and Dates Determined Month to Month. Check at www.wdfw.wa.gov	Min Size 1 1/2", 40, 10 lbs. Combined Total
Littleneck, Manila	All Year	20 Clams, 12 in Aggregate Gaper or Geoducks	Locations, Times and Dates Determined Month to Month. Check at www.wdfw.wa.gov	Min Size 1 1/2", 40, 10 lbs. Combined Total
Purple Varnish, Mahogany	All Year	72 Per Day	Locations, Times and Dates Determined Month to Month. Check at www.wdfw.wa.gov	40, 10 lbs. Combined Total
Mussel	All Year	72	Locations, Times and Dates Determined Month to Month. Check at www.wdfw.wa.gov	10 lbs. in Shell
Oyster	Closed All Year	Oregon Not Permitted	Locations, Times and Dates Determined Month to Month. Check at www.wdfw.wa.gov	18 Shucked, 2 1/5" min

Clamming Locations

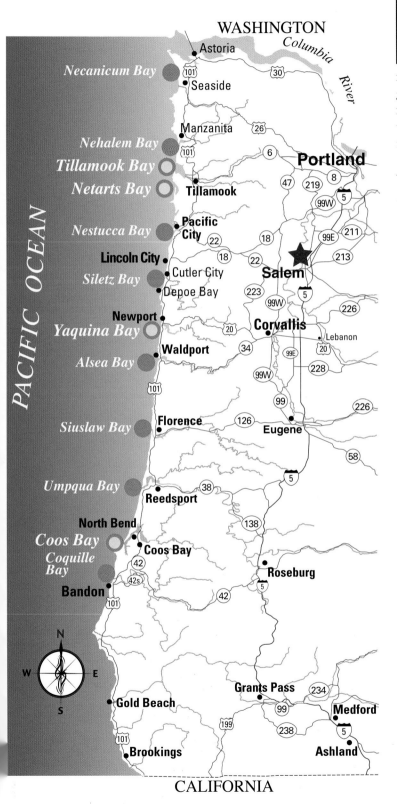

In the old days if you didn't have friends to show you where the clams were, you just didn't go! Today with the internet it's a whole new world. Knowing where to go is so important and I think more people are interested in clamming because it's a lot easier to find out where to go. In addition, with products like Google Earth (available for free on the internet), you can literally zoom down to the earth's surface and see clammers on the beach. Even finding hidden trails and hard-to-find spots becomes easy. Of course Google Earth isn't clamming specific and that's where websites like www.razorclamming.com come into play, we offer clamming-specific maps from all around the Pacific Northwest.

For more information on locations go to www.razorclamming.com/locations where you will find numerous clamming-specific maps (and we are adding more all the time).

You can also go to the Oregon Department of Fish and Wildlife at www.dfw.state.or.us and the Washington Department of Fish and Wildlife at wdfw.wa.gov. Both websites offer numerous maps that they are constantly updating.

Highlighted bays have six or more clam species, Willapa Bay is the only bay with Oysters.

BEST OREGON BAYS

SEASIDE TO CLATSOP SPIT AND COLUMBIA RIVER

Oregon beaches are all publically owned. Drive onto the beach where beach access is noted.

Razor Clam

Softshell

Purple Varnish

OREGON

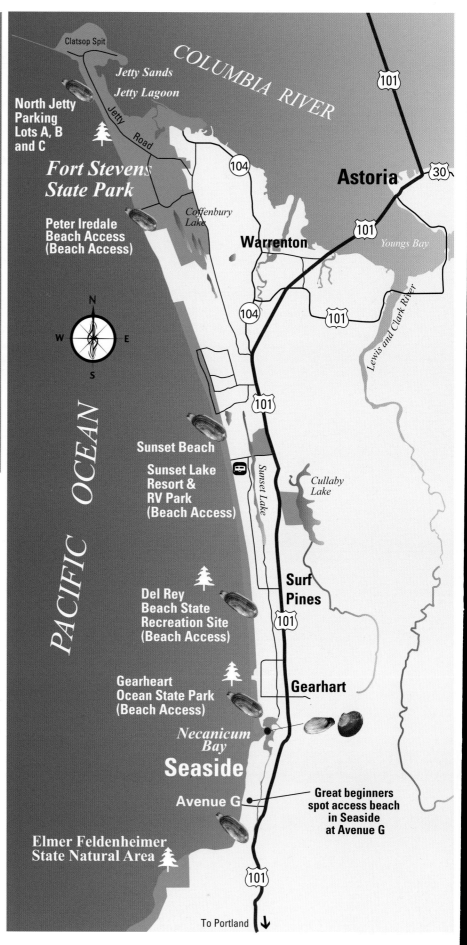

Clatsop Spit

COLUMBIA RIVER

Jetty Sands

Jetty Lagoon

North Jetty Parking Lots A, B and C

Jetty Road

104

Astoria

30

101

Fort Stevens State Park

Coffenbury Lake

Warrenton

101

Youngs Bay

Peter Iredale Beach Access (Beach Access)

104

101

Lewis and Clark River

PACIFIC OCEAN

101

Sunset Beach

Sunset Lake Resort & RV Park (Beach Access)

Sunset Lake

Cullaby Lake

Del Rey Beach State Recreation Site (Beach Access)

Surf Pines

101

Gearheart Ocean State Park (Beach Access)

Gearhart

Necanicum Bay

Seaside

Great beginners spot access beach in Seaside at Avenue G

Avenue G

Elmer Feldenheimer State Natural Area

101

To Portland

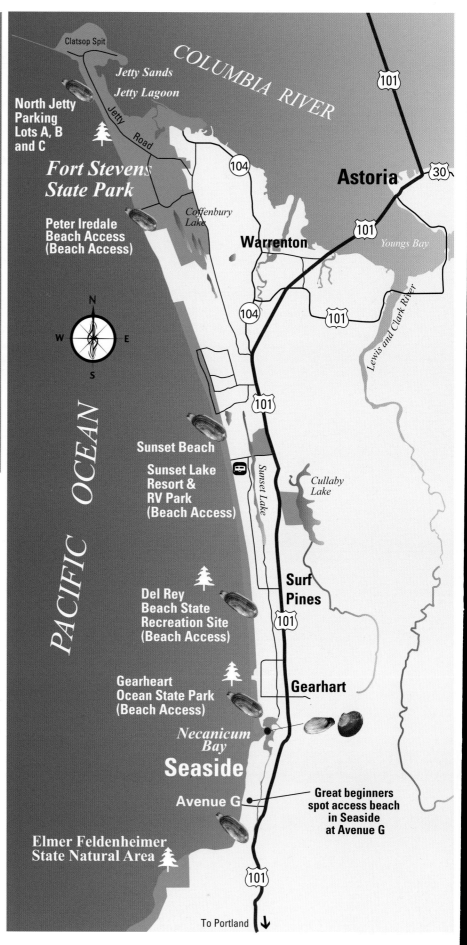

TILLAMOOK BAY

Parking areas mark two great places for beginners; areas in center are boat access only.

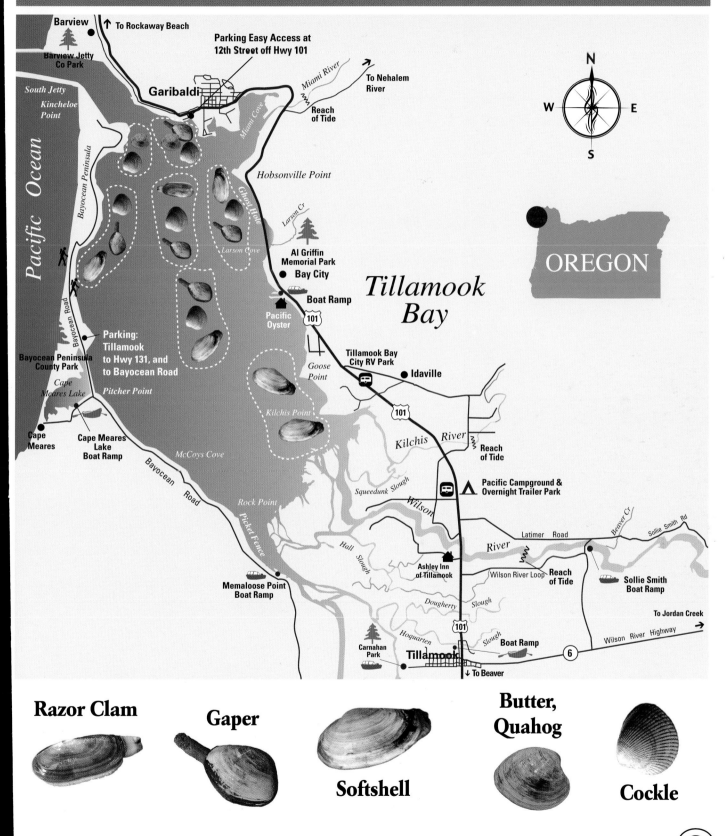

Razor Clam

Gaper

Softshell

Butter, Quahog

Cockle

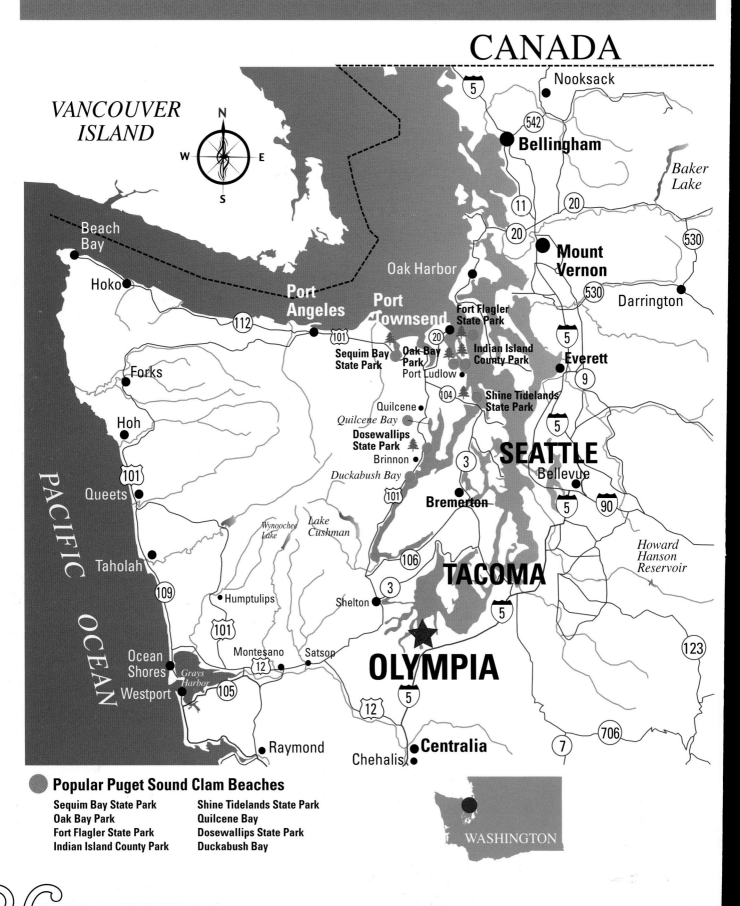

CANADA

VANCOUVER ISLAND

Nooksack

Bellingham

Baker Lake

Mount Vernon

Darrington

Beach Bay

Hoko

Oak Harbor

Port Angeles

Port Townsend

Fort Flagler State Park

Everett

Sequim Bay State Park

Oak Bay Park

Indian Island County Park

Port Ludlow

Forks

Quilcene

Shine Tidelands State Park

Hoh

Quilcene Bay

Dosewallips State Park

Brinnon

SEATTLE

Bellevue

Duckabush Bay

Queets

Bremerton

PACIFIC OCEAN

Wynoochee Lake

Lake Cushman

Howard Hanson Reservoir

Taholah

TACOMA

Humptulips

Shelton

Ocean Shores

Montesano

Satsop

OLYMPIA

Grays Harbor

Westport

Centralia

Raymond

Chehalis

Popular Puget Sound Clam Beaches

Sequim Bay State Park
Oak Bay Park
Fort Flagler State Park
Indian Island County Park

Shine Tidelands State Park
Quilcene Bay
Dosewallips State Park
Duckabush Bay

WASHINGTON

FORT FLAGLER, INDIAN ISLAND & OAK BAY

Great Geoduck clamming! Also part of Washington State's clam enhancement program.

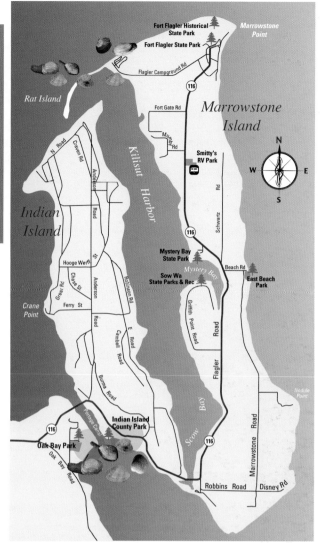

Razor Clam

Gaper

Softshell

Butter, Quahog

Cockle

Purple Varnish

Littleneck, Manila

Geoduck

Clam Enhancement Program

WASHINGTON

To Port Angeles ↑

Dosewallips Rd

Schoolhouse Rd

Brinnon Ln

Brinnon General Store

101

Dosewallips River

Dabob Bay

Dosewallips State Park

Brinnon

↓ To Eldon

101

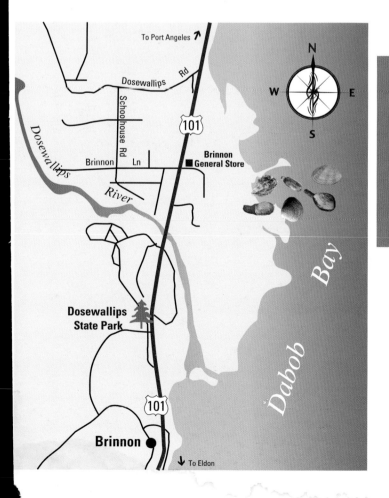

DOSEWALLIPS STATE PARK

Great Manila and Littleneck clamming. Geoducks on -2.0 or better; oysters too!

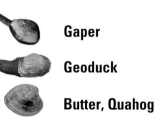

Gaper

Geoduck

Butter, Quahog

Littleneck

Cockle

Oyster

WASHINGTON

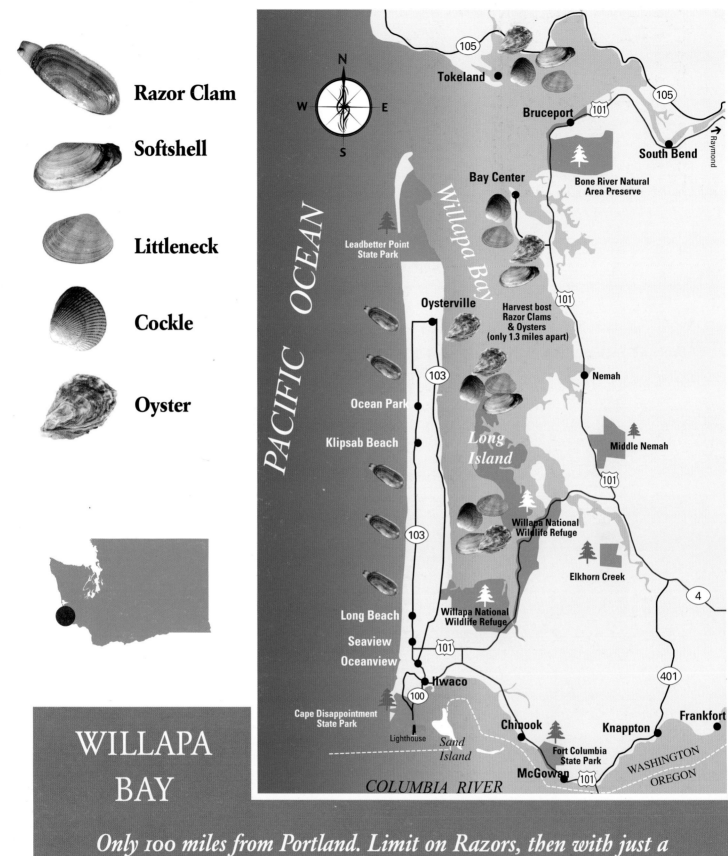

Razor Clam

Softshell

Littleneck

Cockle

Oyster

WILLAPA BAY

Only 100 miles from Portland. Limit on Razors, then with just a short drive limit out on oysters.

Map labels:

PACIFIC OCEAN

COLUMBIA RIVER

Willapa Bay

Long Island

Tokeland

Bruceport

South Bend

Raymond

Bay Center

Bone River Natural Area Preserve

Leadbetter Point State Park

Harvest bost Razor Clams & Oysters (only 1.3 miles apart)

Oysterville

Nemah

Ocean Park

Middle Nemah

Klipsab Beach

Willapa National Wildlife Refuge

Willapa National Wildlife Refuge

Elkhorn Creek

Long Beach

Seaview

Oceanview

Ilwaco

Cape Disappointment State Park

Lighthouse

Sand Island

Chinook

Fort Columbia State Park

Knappton

Frankfort

McGowan

WASHINGTON

OREGON

Route markers: 105, 101, 103, 100, 4, 401